—LOST LINES—
JOINT
RAILWAYS

NIGEL WELBOURN

Ian Allan
PUBLISHING

Contents

First published 2010

ISBN 978 0 7110 3428 0

© Nigel Welbourn 2010

Published by Ian Allan Publishing

an imprint of Ian Allan Publishing Ltd, Hersham, Surrey, KT12 4RG.

Printed in England by Ian Allan Printing Ltd, Hersham, Surrey, KT12 4RG.

Distributed in the United States of America and Canada and by BookMasters Distribution Services

Code: 1006/B2

Visit the Ian Allan Publishing website at www.ianallanpublishing.com

Cover images courtesy of Colour-Rail

Key to maps:

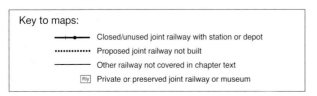

- Closed/unused joint railway with station or depot
- Proposed joint railway not built
- Other railway not covered in chapter text
- Rly Private or preserved joint railway or museum

Mixed Sources
Product group from well-managed forests and other controlled sources
www.fsc.org Cert no. SGS-COC-005526
© 1996 Forest Stewardship Council

Introduction

Joint railways have not always fitted logically into earlier volumes of 'Lost Lines'. This book addresses that situation and considers all of Britain's major closed joint railways from the delightful S&D, the distinctive M&GN and busy CLC, to some of the more obscure, but equally individual and interesting joint railways, lines and stations. All significant closed joint lines are referenced in the text, including those that were light railways, narrow-gauge or tramways. Joint lines were often unique and had distinctive liveries, the yellow ochre of the M&GN, the blue of the S&D and the geranium red of the CDRJC being examples. Equally the design of joint stations and in some cases motive power, rolling stock and staff uniforms made a statement that these were individual railways — although many also used the rolling stock and locomotives of the companies that worked them.

It could be argued that some joint lines should have never been built. Equally, because they were run not by a single railway company but by a joint committee, many lines suffered from a lack of long-term planning and investment, and there have been widespread closures. Joint railways were a fascinating, inventive and very British product of the pre-nationalised railway network and proved that even the fiercest rivals could work amicably together. With the exception of the CDRJC, which survived until 1960, the joint railway ceased to exist upon the nationalisation of the railways in 1948. Yet many intriguing and unusual remains are still to be found, both in the remotest rural areas and in the heart of great cities.

Abbreviations

AJ	Axholme Joint Railway
AN	Ashby & Nuneaton Joint Railway
CLC	Cheshire Lines Committee
CDRJC	County Donegal Railways Joint Committee
GC&NS	Great Central & North Staffordshire Joint Railway
GN&GE	Great Northern & Great Eastern Joint Committee
H&O	Halifax & Ovenden Junction Railway
MetGC	Metropolitan & Great Central Joint Committee
M&GN	Midland & Great Northern Joint Railway
N&S	Norfolk & Suffolk Joint Railway
OAGB	Oldham, Ashton-under-Lyne & Guide Bridge Junction Railway
PWR	Preston & Wyre Joint Railway
P&W	Portpatrick & Wigtownshire Joint Railway
S&D	Somerset & Dorset Joint Railway (and all later references to line)
S&W	Severn & Wye Joint Railway
SYJ	South Yorkshire Joint Railway
WP	Weymouth & Portland Joint Railway
WCE	Whitehaven, Cleator & Egremont Railway

Below: The heyday of the joint railway. A Johnson 0-6-0 in M&GN livery at Melton Constable, once known as the 'Crewe of North Norfolk', on 26 September 1936. No 71 seen here was fitted with a larger Belpaire boiler in 1921 and lasted well after the LNER takeover of the M&GN, not being withdrawn until 1943. All but a short section of this most extensive former joint railway closed to passengers in February 1959, being the first major rail closure in Britain. *J. Adams*

1 Historical background

The joint railway was predominantly (although not exclusively) a British device for providing ownership or operation of a line by more than one railway company. The origins of joint railways and lines varied, but a number of underlying principles can be identified. These included allowing the expansion of one railway into the traditional territory of another railway. They sometimes came about when company boundaries met and no one railway was seen as the natural partner to cover a potential area, or source of traffic. They were on occasion created as a means of settling differences over proposed new routes of rival railways. Easing heavy traffic flows, or allowing the

cost of expensive infrastructure to be shared, were also reasons to join together. After 1900, in particular, over-capacity on parts of the railway system increasingly resulted in commercial expediency, bringing hitherto fierce rivals cordially together in the operation of joint lines.

The Lancashire & Yorkshire and London & North Western railways came together in the 1840s to lease the Preston & Wyre Railway. Other joint lines followed, and they continued to be created by the 'Big Four' (established by the 1923 Grouping) right up to the 1930s. In several instances the joint line was the result of the merger of earlier individual smaller

Left: Joint railways often developed by the merger of earlier independent lines. This early view of Spetisbury, south of Blandford Forum, was on the first section of the Dorset Central Railway that opened in 1860 and became part of the S&D joint line in 1876. Note the disc-and-crossbar signal, at clear, on the single line. The station became an unstaffed halt in 1934 and closed in 1956, the buildings being demolished in the early 1960s. *Ian Allan Library*

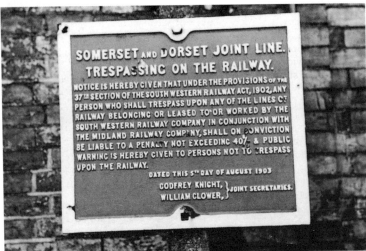

Left: S&D cast-iron sign at Blandford Forum, photographed on 25 September 1965. *E. Wilmhurst*

railways that were later incorporated into a joint railway company.

The distinct Midland & Great Northern, that pushed its tentacles out from the Midlands to the Norfolk coast, was the largest joint railway, followed by the Cheshire Lines Committee. The delightful Somerset & Dorset over the Mendip Hills and the Great Northern & Great Eastern linking East Anglia with the North each comprised more than 100 miles of line, but several of the smaller joint lines were short strategic links, some less than two miles in length.

Countless combinations of railway companies working jointly together developed, but the main protagonist was the Midland, which had interests in more than 20 joint lines throughout Britain, covering over 850 miles, including the M&GN, CLC, S&D and CDRJC, followed by the London & North Western and the Great Western, each with over a dozen joint-line arrangements. The Great Central, Great Northern, Caledonian, Lancashire & Yorkshire and North Eastern railways all had involvement in up to half a dozen joint lines. In many cases more than two companies were involved, five being the maximum.

The *modus operandi* of joint lines varied. Some, such as the M&GN, S&D and CDRJC, were individual companies, with their own assets, locomotives, stock and coats of arms — in effect independent railways. Others, such as the CLC, had no main-line locomotives of their own. Several, such as the GN&GE, were not separate railway companies but lines with access for the railways concerned, while some, such as the Metropolitan Railway, leased sections of their lines to joint committees; such lines were run by joint managing committees comprising directors of the owning companies. Typically members would receive payment, there would often be a chair, and decisions would be taken by a majority vote. Costs and receipts would be shared by agreement between the railway companies involved.

Above: A handsome Beyer Peacock 4-4-0, No 23, delivered to the M&GN in 1882. It is seen here arriving at Weybourne, with a mixed rake of coaches, including those from the owning companies. The locomotive was scrapped in 1937, giving a clue to the latest date of this view. Note also the station fencing, a distinctive feature throughout the M&GN. *Ian Allan Library*

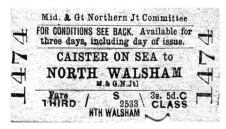

Below: M&GN cast-iron sign at Bourne, photographed on 20 June 1965. *P. Wells*

Left: The huge ex-CLC Central Manchester goods depot and arches over the canal at Watson Street and Peter Street, pictured on 23 August 1938. This was one of several enormous and prominently branded goods warehouses that were scattered across the CLC network. The building was damaged during World War 2, and the ruins were demolished in 1978.
Ian Allan Library

Right: Gateacre for Woolton, on the CLC North Liverpool line, at the dawn of the last century. Note the distinctive colouring of the platform canopy valances. Passenger services would cease in April 1972, and freight by 1975. The station has been demolished, but the trackbed is now used as part of the Liverpool Loop Line footpath/cycleway.
Ian Allan Library

Left: The ex-GC&NS Joint Railway, with the 4.28pm Manchester London Road–Macclesfield train, hauled by ex-GCR Robinson Class C13 4-4-2T No 67422, arriving at the oil-lit Middlewood High Level station. This locomotive was among the earlier examples of its type to be withdrawn, in September 1954, dating this view to the early 1950s. The line closed in January 1970.
H. Bryant

There was just one joint narrow-gauge railway, the CDRJC, serving the remote and sparsely populated county of Donegal, in Ireland. There were two joint light railways, in remote areas of Scotland and Lincolnshire. There were also two joint railway-owned passenger tramways, to Brill in Buckinghamshire and at Weymouth.

There were a couple of dozen jointly owned stations, mainly in big cities, but with a rural scattering elsewhere from Ashbourne to Chard. There were joint locomotive sheds at Fratton and Aberdeen, and jointly owned railway hotels at Preston and Perth, while sailings from Highbridge, Stranraer and Balloch were once operated by jointly owned steamers. There was also jointly owned passenger stock, used mainly between England and Scotland. Prior to 1923 some 70 or so lines, representing about 10% of the network, were jointly operated.

In 1899 a managing committee was set up to oversee a working union of the South Eastern Railway and London, Chatham & Dover Railway, but legally they remained separate companies. The same applied to the LNWR's interest in the nominally independent Greenore Railway in Ireland, where six of the eight directors were also directors of the LNWR, but this was not a formally operated joint railway.

In 1909 the GNR and GCR planned a joint arrangement, which the GER proposed to join, but the prospect of prolonged parliamentary debate resulted in the withdrawal of the proposal. In some cases the potential complications of joint railways were explicitly avoided, lines of individual companies running in parallel, or running powers of one company being granted over another's line — without any question of ownership.

In order to prevent over-complication, or commercial inequity, the Grouping of railway companies into the 'Big Four' in 1923 left some of the joint railways unaltered. Most of the pre-Grouping names of joint railways were also retained, although where the title made reference to 'LNW' or 'Midland' this was generally altered to 'LMS'. However, the majority of joint lines that found themselves entirely within the territory of one of the 'Big Four' lost their identities, their shares being transferred to the LNER, LMS, GWR or SR as appropriate.

Other joint committees continued with the new owners, but the LMS and LNER created new committees to deal with groups of lines operated jointly by the two companies. The CLC became two-thirds owned by the LMS and one-third by the LNER but remained as a separate operating company. The S&D became vested jointly in the LMS and SR, while the M&GN, after a period of joint LMS/LNER operation, was administered wholly by the latter from 1936. The last joint line to be constructed was the Mid Nottinghamshire, opened by the LMS and LNER in 1932 to serve a coal-mining district north of Nottingham.

Above: GC&NS Joint Railway cast-iron notice at High Lane station, between Rose Hill (Marple) and Macclesfield. *I. Smith*

The nationalisation and unification of Britain's railways in 1948 saw the end of the traditional joint lines (although this did not apply to the CDRJC in the north west of Ireland). It also raised new issues, as, in the new regional structure, some formerly joint lines were known as 'penetrating lines' or did not fall sensibly within any one Region. Moreover, although the formation of BR had spelled the end of the joint railway, 'CLC' continued to appear on coaches, tickets and signs for many years after nationalisation.

Joint lines were sometimes built where it was not commercially viable for a railway to construct its own line. Short stretches had closed as early as the 1870s, but considerable sections were early candidates for closure under the unified BR, and those remaining were not exempt from the Beeching 'axe' of the 1960s. Today a majority of the formerly joint lines are closed, but lengthy sections remain open.

Above: Staff pose with a GWR 2-4-0T 'Metro Tank' at the Hotwells terminus, at Clifton on the GW & Midland Joint Railway, in the 1890s. Opened in 1864 as the Bristol Port & Pier Railway, the line ran along the north bank of the Avon from beneath the suspension bridge to Avonmouth. The Portway road was built over the Sea Mills–Hotwells section of the joint line following closure of the latter in September 1921. *R. Winstone*

Right: Rubery station, on the one-time GW & Midland Halesowen Railway, photographed in 1957 — after the withdrawal of regular passenger services (in 1919) but before the cessation of freight (in 1964). The down starter seen here had a GWR signal arm and an MR post. There were few joint lines in the West Midlands. The Halesowen Railway is described in detail in *Lost Lines: Birmingham and the Black Country*. *Ian Allan Library*

Above: A neat Parkend station in the Dean Forest, on the Severn & Wye Joint Railway, in 1910. Regular passenger services ended in 1929, but freight survived much longer, until 1976. Today the Parkend–Lydney Junction section of line is operated by the Dean Forest Railway. *Ian Allan Library*

Below: CDRJC railcar No 12 on the Ballyshannon branch in June 1949. The CDRJC took delivery of this railcar in 1934. It combined a Walkers diesel-powered bogie, built in Wigan, with a coach body built by the GNR(I) at Dundalk. The railcars represented an economical means of providing passenger services, and their usefulness could be increased by an ability to haul trailers, as seen here. The Joint Committee's pioneering work in the use of diesel railcars prolonged the life of the railway by several years. *P. B. Whitehouse*

Left: The view east at Verney Junction, a joint LNWR/MetGC station, after closure of the line to Quainton Road in 1956. The platform on the far right was used by MetGC trains and was controlled originally by Met-style signals, while the platform on the left was originally protected by LNWR-style signals. *R. Sexton*

Left: Class 33 No 6506, in BR corporate livery, propels a demolition train past Corfe Mullen on 4 April 1970. The trackbed of the erstwhile connection to Wimborne can be seen in the background. Although the S&D through line to Wimborne closed to passengers in July 1920 and to freight in June 1933 a section from Corfe Mullen to Carter's siding remained open for freight until September 1959. *J. Bird*

Above right: Balloch Pier with the final electric train, on 29 September 1986. The Dumbarton–Balloch Pier line was the joint property of the NBR and CR and later became an LMS/LNER joint railway, one of the few in Scotland to remain in joint ownership after the 1923 Grouping. Most trains terminated at Balloch Central, but some ran through to the pier until this short overgrown section was closed, being one of the later closures of a former joint line. *C. Berry*

Right: An arched iron lattice bridge carrying a farm track over the one-time Whitehaven, Cleator & Egremont Railway, operated jointly by the Furness and London & North Western railways. The photograph was taken north of Woodend station, in the direction of Moor Row, in July 2009. The WCE is one of a number of formerly joint railways to have been closed in their entirety. *Author*

2 A geographical perspective

Although found in England, Wales, Scotland and Ireland, joint railways were not evenly distributed throughout the United Kingdom. Most were found in industrial areas, notably in the coal-mining regions of Lancashire and Yorkshire, and the Cheshire Lines Committee, in particular, was an important player in the North West.

Joint ownership was also to be found at several urban stations, and those closed include the Central stations at Liverpool, Manchester and Leeds, as well as Birkenhead Woodside and Nottingham Victoria. In rural areas joint lines once provided busy freight routes, particularly for coal and iron ore, while a random selection of smaller joint stations was also to be found. Joint lines were on occasion used as a mechanism to share the costs of estuary crossings, such as the Forth and Severn bridges and even the railway pier at Ryde.

In London and the South East there were few joint railways, although the line to the Isle of Portland was the most southerly joint line in Britain, and at one time joint lines could also be found on the Isle of Wight and the Isle of Axholme. Certainly in recent times the most-photographed former joint railway was the evocative S&D, with its long and often single line, snaking through the beautiful Mendip Hills.

Left: The CLC served the industrial North West. Here, on 20 June 1964, Class B1 4-6-0 No 61394 from Canklow (41D) shed is seen at Stockport Tiviot Dale on a train to Sheffield, via Chinley. Note the unique arched footbridge. Passenger closure came in January 1967, demolition of most of the station being effected by the following year. Freight trains continued to run through the site until 1982, but the track was lifted in 1986, and today no trace of the station remains. *S. Staddow*

Below left: The M&GN extended eastward to Great Yarmouth, which was a major East Coast herring port and holiday resort. Great Yarmouth Beach station is seen here on 28 May 1937, with ex-M&GN 0-6-0T No 16, dating from 1905, acting as the station pilot. The station was located less than 200yd from the sandy beach and North Sea. A later view of this locomotive can be found at Chapter 12. *H. C. Casserley.*

Above right: The CDRJC station at Killybegs, viewed in the direction of the buffer-stops and harbour, on 4 September 1957. Being located beside the Atlantic Ocean, it was provided with an overall roof to afford passengers protection from westerly gales. Opened in August 1893, the deep-water harbour on the west coast of Ireland was at one time considered as a possible port for transatlantic liners. The station closed in December 1959 and was subsequently demolished and bulldozed into the sea. *N. Simmons*

Equal to the S&D in terms of length, the M&GN pushed its way eastward from the Midlands to the holiday areas of the Norfolk coast, passing through fenland countryside, where substantial bridges were required over the rivers Ouse and Nene. At Breydon, meanwhile, the Norfolk & Suffolk line (a joint venture between the Great Eastern and the already joint M&GN!) was forced to cross an arm of the Norfolk Broads via an M&GN line to reach Lowestoft, on the most easterly part of the British coast.

There were few joint railways in the West Midlands and only a limited number in the dense coalfield network of South Wales, but lost joint LNW and GW branches are to be found in the Welsh borders. In Scotland there were some joint lines around Glasgow, but the Carmyllie branch of the Dundee & Arbroath Joint Railway was the most northerly joint line in Britain. The longest Scottish joint line crossed a desolate and beautiful part of Dumfries and Galloway

to provide links with Ireland. There was one joint narrow-gauge line in Ireland, and a CDRJC branch once ran to the Atlantic coast at Killybegs. Elsewhere in the Republic of Ireland there was just one short section of joint passenger line, at Waterford.

Joint railways were found in other parts of the world, although operating procedures and 'trackage' (running) rights were organised in different ways. Interesting examples included the Union stations in America: the largest, in Washington DC, was controlled by a joint management board until it was taken over by a non-profit-making organisation not dissimilar to Network Rail.

This book considers only lost joint railways, starting in the South and travelling north to Scotland and Ireland. All lines of more than two miles in length are mentioned in the text, although a few have already been described in detail in other volumes in this series.

Right: A view of the single line over the 22-span Severn Bridge, looking towards Lydney and the Forest of Dean. The ex-S&W bridge was 4,162ft (1,268m) long and 70ft (21.3m) high. The photograph is undated but was taken before two spans crashed into the estuary below, after a tanker barge demolished one of the river piers on a foggy night in 1960. Other spans were deformed by the accident, and demolition of the entire bridge began in 1965. *M. Windeatt*

Above: Snow and steam on the S&D on 6 March 1965 after a blizzard. BR Standard Class 4 2-6-4T No 80037 approaches Masbury Summit on the crest of the Mendips, some 811ft above sea level, with the 08.15 Bath–Templecombe local. In winter the exposed cutting here was liable to fill with drifting snow, blocking the line. *M. Fox*

Below: A Stranraer–Carlisle boat train on the 'Port Road', hauled by 'Black Five' 4-6-0 No 44996, crossing the three-span bow-string viaduct over Loch Ken, near Parton station, on 11 June 1963. Note the brackets on top of the metal arches, to carry telephone wires. The viaduct survives. *Derek Cross*

③ Somerset & Dorset Joint Railway

The S&D became something of a legend in its own lifetime and was probably the best loved of all the joint lines. It developed to become a distinctive and evocative railway, with its famous blue livery, specially designed locomotives and dark-green corduroy uniforms. In later years the image of long holiday trains struggling up the formidable gradients over the scenic Mendip Hills gave the line lasting fascination and recognition.

The line could trace its origins to the broad-gauge Somerset Central Railway, opened between Highbridge and Glastonbury in August 1854, while the standard-gauge Dorset Central Railway opened the Wimborne–Blandford section in November 1860 and the Templecombe–Cole section in February 1862. The Somerset Central also reached Cole in 1862, and in that year the two amalgamated to form the Somerset & Dorset Railway. With leave to convert the broad-gauge section to standard gauge, the railway provided a through route between Burnham-on-Sea and Wimborne and had running powers over the LSWR line to Poole and Bournemouth.

The coastal traffic at Burnham did not prosper, and the line, which passed through a sparsely populated rural area, did not prove an instant success. As a consequence the S&D gambled everything on building a spectacular, heavily graded (and expensive) 26-mile line across the Mendip Hills from Evercreech to Bath. This new line opened in July 1874 but proved a serious strain on finances, and the S&D was forced to grant a long lease to the LSW and Midland railways,

in 1876 becoming the S&D Joint Railway. A Joint Committee was established, and a secretary and general manager were appointed. Together with further links to Wells and Bridgwater the Bath–Broadstone and Evercreech Junction–Burnham lines created a 105-mile network, making the S&D the country's fourth-longest joint line in terms of route mileage.

Traffic grew significantly on the Bath line, which provided a convenient route for holidaymakers, as well as for freight, from the Midlands and North to and from Bournemouth and the South Coast and consequently developed as the main line. From 1883 the Corfe Mullen–Broadstone cut-off allowed direct running to Poole and Bournemouth without reversal at

Below: Bath Green Park, the MR-built northern terminus of the S&D, bustling with activity one afternoon in the late 1950s. Ex-LMS Class 2P 4-4-0 No 40697 sets out for Bournemouth with the 4.25pm while ex-MR Class 2P 4-4-0 No 40509 waits in one of the middle roads with the 4.37pm down local; on the right Ivatt 2-6-2T No 41240 prepares to amble off to the sheds after bringing in a local from Bristol. Following closure of the station in March 1966 the elegant listed building was eventually (in 1979) converted for retail use. *Ivo Peters*

Left: Climbing the steep (1-in-50) single line out of Bath towards the restricted bore of the 447yd (409m) Devonshire Tunnel, ex-LMS Class 4F 0-6-0 No 44422 sets out after the 'Pines Express' with the 3.20pm Bristol–Templecombe local on 16 June 1961. The locomotive has been preserved, while the bridge also survives. The trackbed here is now used as a footpath. *C. Walker*

Right: S&D crest, combining the arms of Bath (left) and the seal of Dorchester.

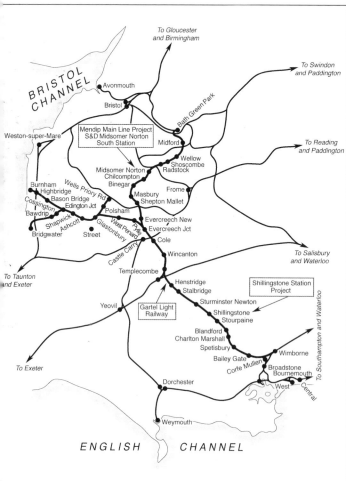

Wimborne. Through long-distance freight — particularly coal but also beer, together with local agricultural produce — developed along the line. Coal and stone trains also originated from the Mendips themselves, and in the line's heyday the volume of traffic was such that freight trains ran throughout the night.

Although much of the main line was doubled, some 22 miles remained single track. It had been the intention to double the main line throughout, but Alfred Whitaker's automatic tablet-exchanging apparatus, brought into operation in 1904, was so successful in accelerating traffic that sections through the Mendips remained single. The company became jointly vested in the LMS and SR at the Grouping in 1923. Some economies were made, halts were added, but the railway retained its title, and a spirit of individuality remained. In 1948 the S&D was assigned initially to the Southern Region of BR, and few at that time would have forecast the devastating effect that nationalisation would ultimately have on this busy railway.

Left: Midford signalbox, with Whitaker's tablet-exchange apparatus, in 1923. The arm of the apparatus is turned at right angles to the line ready for use, the tablet to be exchanged being in a leather pouch with a steel ring above, which engaged with a combined deliverer/receiver on the locomotive. The apparatus was a well-tried feature of single-line sections of the S&D and could be used at speed. The internal equipment and tablet apparatus from Midford signalbox have been preserved at Washford station, on the West Somerset Railway, while the long station platform seen here behind the signalbox still survives at Midford. *Ian Allan Library*

Above: The ex-GWR Camerton branch passed under Midford Viaduct and was the location for the 1952 film *The Titfield Thunderbolt*. The last working on the branch, on 30 June 1958, was a demolition train, seen here being hauled by ex-GWR '57xx' 0-6-0PT No 9628. Passing on the S&D viaduct above is a down freight hauled by BR Standard Class 5 4-6-0 No 73116. *Ivo Peters*

Above: Ex-LMS Class 4F 0-6-0 No 44561 at Writhlington with a late-afternoon Templecombe–Bath train *c*1955. At one time the Somerset Coalfield, evidence of which is visible here, generated much business for the railway; indeed, the colliery provided the final freight traffic on the S&D, this continuing until November 1973. *Derek Cross*

Left: S&D 2-8-0 No 53807, a Fowler-designed locomotive built at Derby, entering Radstock North with the 7am Templecombe–Bath on 15 August 1959. The only serious accident in the line's 111-year history occurred near here in 1876, when there was a head-on collision on the then single line, killing 15 passengers. The Midford–Radstock section was doubled in the years 1892-4. *F. Saunders*

Above: Ex-LMS Class 2P 4-4-0 No 40698 arrives at Midsomer Norton South, amid its hanging baskets and gas lamps, with a Templecombe–Bath local in August 1958. Opened in July 1874, the station lost its goods facilities in June 1964, and passenger services were withdrawn in March 1966. The S&D Railway Heritage Trust has since taken over the station. *Derek Cross*

Below: S&D and LSWR notices at Midsomer Norton South in 1959. *M. Cornick*

SOUTHERN AND LONDON, MIDLAND & SCOTTISH RAILWAY COMPANIES
(SOMERSET AND DORSET JOINT RAILWAY)

L.&S.W.R.
BEWARE OF TRAINS

SOMERSET AND DORSET JOINT LINE.
TRESPASSING ON THE RAILWAY.
NOTICE IS HEREBY GIVEN THAT UNDER THE PROVISIONS OF THE 37th SECTION OF THE SOUTH WESTERN RAILWAY ACT, 1902, ANY PERSON WHO SHALL TRESPASS UPON ANY OF THE LINES OF RAILWAY BELONGING OR LEASED TO OR WORKED BY THE SOUTH WESTERN RAILWAY COMPANY IN CONJUNCTION WITH THE MIDLAND RAILWAY COMPANY, SHALL ON CONVICTION BE LIABLE TO A PENALTY NOT EXCEEDING 40/- & PUBLIC WARNING IS HEREBY GIVEN TO PERSONS NOT TO TRESPASS UPON THE RAILWAY.
DATED THIS 5th DAY OF AUGUST 1903
GODFREY KNIGHT, } JOINT SECRETARIES.
WILLIAM CLOWER,

Above: Ex-LMS Class 2P 4-4-0 No 40700, the last locomotive in the series, emerges from Winsor Hill Tunnel on recently re-ballasted track with a Bath–Templecombe local in August 1960. The two single-line tunnels were cut through solid rock, the original 'down' tunnel being 242yd (221m) long, and the 'up' tunnel, added when the line was doubled in 1892, 132yd (120m) long. *Derek Cross*

Left: The 12.35pm Bath–Evercreech Junction freight running on descending grade over Prestleigh Viaduct. The undated photograph was taken from one of the extra brake vans attached, to the already lengthy train, for members of the Bath Railway Society. *Ivo Peters*

Above: BR Standard Class 3MT 2-6-2T No 82002 heads the afternoon Templecombe–Bailey Gate stopping train away from Templecombe station towards the junction 'box on 28 June 1962. At the junction the train will reverse and, headed by sister locomotive No 82001 (seen here at the rear) running bunker-first, make its way south over the single-line spur on the left. The need for such complex manœuvrings might have been avoided had the joint committee set aside more funds for investment in the line. *Derek Cross*

Right: Ex-LMS Class 4F 0-6-0 No 44422 (now preserved) shunting just north of Blandford Forum station on 23 September 1964. The line to the south had been doubled in 1901, but the section to Templecombe remained single, with four passing loops. The station at Blandford ('Forum' was added in 1953), once the terminus of the Dorset Central Railway, would be demolished after closure. To quote a couple of lines from the song 'The Slow Train' by Flanders and Swann, 'No more will I go to Blandford Forum … On the slow train from Midsomer Norton'. *P. Walnes*

21

4 Branch line to Burnham

Once the Somerset Central Railway had opened the Glastonbury–Highbridge line in 1854 the value of an extension to Burnham-on-Sea was recognised, and this 1¾-mile line opened in May 1858. Glastonbury became a junction for Wells the following year, and by 1862 the plan to develop Burnham as a rail-served port on a strategic South Wales–South Coast route, with links to France, had come to fruition.

As part of this plan, track ran onto a stone pier more than 900ft (278m) long, built into the Bristol Channel at Burnham. The Burnham Tidal Harbour & Railway Co was established, as a subsidiary of the S&D, and a variety of vessels provided connections with Cardiff and South Wales. Connecting trains to Poole were provided from Burnham, but passenger traffic did not meet expectations. Coal was also increasingly exported directly from South Wales ports, and the opening of the Severn Tunnel also reduced traffic using Burnham.

The Bath extension opened in 1874 and changed the emphasis of working, Burnham becoming the end of a branch from Evercreech Junction, while the opening in 1890 of the Edington Junction–Bridgwater line saw the Burnham line relegated further, as a branch from this junction. Burnham also had limitations as a resort, whereas Highbridge proved to be a safer harbour. Consequently in the 1880s Highbridge Wharf replaced the pier at Burnham as the main port, although pleasure steamers used Burnham until World War 1.

Whilst this all led to the decline of long-distance traffic from Burnham, prior to the outbreak of World War 1 a local push-pull shuttle service, of some 18 trains in each direction, developed between Highbridge and Burnham, eight trains in each direction being extended to Edington Junction. Seaside specials were also run, and an excursion platform was added at Burnham.

After the LMS and SR had taken over operation a single Burnham–Bournemouth express was reintroduced in 1924. However, the 1930s saw a further decline in the use of the branch, and the original S&D shipping service was wound up. The railway works at nearby Highbridge, which undertook mainly locomotive repairs and carriage and wagon building, also closed in May 1930. Apart from being used for stores during World War 2 the works remained empty; the buildings were partly demolished in 1970 and had disappeared altogether by 1980.

In October 1951 the Burnham–Highbridge section lost its regular passenger service, although summer excursions used the line until September 1962. Complete closure to Burnham was effected in May 1963. A scanty service was provided on the remaining Highbridge–Evercreech Junction section, and this survived until the end of the S&D in March 1966. The Highbridge–Bason Bridge section remained for freight until October 1972.

Although the line was lifted after closure, and many of the structures were demolished, numerous remains can still be found. The hotel and stone jetty at Burnham are still extant, as is the station building at Edington Junction, while at Glastonbury the re-sited island platform canopy survives. Further traces can be found at Ashcott, West Pennard, Pylle and Evercreech Junction stations, while several railway-crossing houses have also survived, and stretches of the trackbed are now used as footpaths.

Left: Evercreech Junction, with Ivatt '2MT' 2-6-2T No 41296 heading the 5.5pm to Highbridge, on 21 May 1965. It is perhaps surprising that no bay platform was ever built for the branch. The width between the platforms was an inheritance from the original broad-gauge days. The station was in an isolated position but became a key point on the S&D for attaching banking engines, taking on water and making connections to what became the branch to Burnham. *R. Roberts*

Left: A general view of the stone-built West Pennard station, with an ex-MR Johnson 0-6-0, No 43419, leaving with an up local goods. When trains stalled on nearby Pylle Bank they were divided, and part of the train would be shunted into the siding here. *C. Maggs*

Above: Glastonbury & Street station once boasted a bookstall and refreshment room. The outer face of the down platform was used by Wells trains until these were withdrawn in October 1951. This view, recorded on 13 August 1957, features ex-MR Class 3F 0-6-0 No 43248 with the 4pm Highbridge–Evercreech Junction. The station was demolished after closure in 1966, but the island platform canopy has been re-erected elsewhere in England's smallest city. *J. Ainslie*

Above: Ex-MR 0-4-4T No 58046 on the single-coach Glastonbury–Wells train, in the sidings at the S&D Wells Priory Road station in May 1950, a year before closure. Not until 1934 did GWR trains stop at the S&D station, having previously run straight through to reach their own station at nearby Tucker Street. Both passenger-station buildings would be demolished after closure. *J. Mills*

Right: Ex-MR Class 3F 0-6-0 No 43248 enters Shapwick station on 14 January 1958 with the 1.15pm Evercreech Junction–Highbridge passenger train. Shapwick was the location of a block post and crossing-place on the single-line branch, and the signalbox also controlled the level crossing on the old turnpike road. Note the station buildings, of wooden construction. *J. Ainslie*

Left: Until closure of the line to Bridgwater the station at Edington Burtle was known as Edington Junction. The passenger service to Bridgwater, which used a bay on the up platform, was withdrawn in December 1952 (at which time the loop and signalbox were removed, freight traffic ceasing in October 1954. The condition of the platform seen here on the right suggests the photograph was taken after the junction was removed. The station was to close in 1966, but the building survives in private ownership. *C. Maggs*

Left: Ex-GWR '2251' 0-6-0 No 3218 near Catcott with the 4pm local train from Highbridge in October 1964. This flat moorland area known as the Somerset Levels was created by draining marshland, the South Drain being seen here in the foreground. Early plans for a ship canal linking Burnham with the English Channel were abandoned when the railway proposed a similar route. *Ivo Peters*

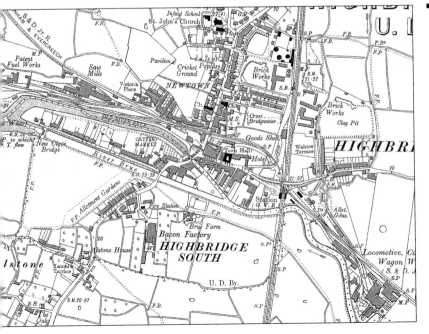

Left: Highbridge in 1930. The works closed in May of that year, but the wharf sidings would remain in use until November 1964.
Crown copyright

Above: Highbridge station *c*1960, with the S&D platform in the foreground and (right) 'A' signalbox, used to control the crossing of the Bristol–Taunton line; 'B' signalbox, of standard GWR design, can be seen in the distance. The one-time S&D station buildings, out of view to the right, have since been demolished. *C. Maggs*

Below: Burnham-on-Sea in August 1959, with a Saturdays-only local train ready to depart for Evercreech Junction behind ex-MR Class 3F 0-6-0 No 43436. Regular passenger services to/from Highbridge were withdrawn in October 1951, but passenger excursions continued to use the station during the summer months until September 1962. The station buildings were demolished after closure, and a road now runs through this location. *G. Bannister*

Above: The SR-style concrete footbridge still survives at the remaining Highbridge station and is seen here on 11 March 2009. However, the section that extended over the S&D lines has been removed, and what was once the top of the staircase providing access to the S&D station platforms bricked up. *Author*

Below: The line beyond Burnham station ran onto a long stone pier constructed by local entrepreneur George Reed, a director of the railway. It was built to serve passenger and commercial traffic from South Wales. Burnham was once even advertised as 'The Gateway to the Continent' because of its links to Poole and the ferry to Le Havre. Most of the jetty survives, and part of it is seen here, on 11 March 2009, in front of the former hotel known once again as the Reed Arms. *Author*

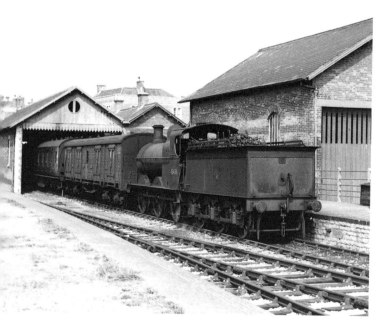

5 The Pines Express

One of the most famous and evocatively named long-distance express trains was the 'Pines Express', which for years was inextricably linked to the S&D main line. Expresses began to use the route before World War 1, originating from northern cities with names such as the 'Bournemouth Express' and returning as the 'North Express'.

Presaging the introduction of the 'Pines Express', the improved timetable effective from October 1910 included a through, year-round restaurant-car service between Bournemouth and Manchester, known unofficially as 'The Diner'. The 'Pines Express' was formally introduced on 26 September 1927, its splendidly romantic title being derived from the numerous pine trees to be found in Poole and Bournemouth.

Operation of the 'Pines Express' was curtailed during World War 2 but effectively recommenced in October 1946 and now included a Sheffield portion, which at weekends during the summer ran as a separate train. The 'Express' name was restored in 1949, but the journey time was still slower than it had been prewar. However, it became the flagship train on the line and the best known of all the expresses using the S&D. In the early 1950s holiday traffic over the route reached its peak, and lengthy summer trains required banking on the steep grades over the Mendips. While booked speeds on the climb to the summit at Masbury were below 30mph, for steam locomotives in charge of heavy trains this represented a hard slog, on gradients as steep as 1 in 50.

The S&D main line was used so heavily that at peak periods in the summer season relief 'Pines' were required, and for many years the line was the principal holiday route between the Midlands and North West and the South Coast. However, by the late 1950s holiday patterns were changing, and although there remained periods of intense activity during peak summer weekends the number of express trains was reduced at other times to the 'Pines Express' and a couple of semi-fast Bristol–Bournemouth expresses — a shadow of the level of service once provided. In later years the 'Pines' even called at Evercreech New.

The death-knell for the line was sounded in 1962 when it was announced that, from the winter timetable, the 'Pines Express', along with other express workings to and from the South Coast, was to be diverted via Oxford and Basingstoke. Hauled by the immaculate *Evening Star*, the 'Pines Express' ran over the S&D for the last time on 8 September. Large crowds turned out to witness this sad event, which proved to be a foretaste of the fate that awaited the line itself. However, for a while after the train's diversion, 'ghost' connections with the 'Pines Express' were nonsensically retained on the S&D!

In March 1967, coinciding with electrification of the West Coast main line as far as Manchester and the closure to main-line services of Birmingham Snow Hill station, the 'Pines Express' was discontinued altogether. However, the name lives on, proving popular for railtours organised by railway-preservation societies.

**THE PINES EXPRESS" EVERCREECH JUNCTION >>>>
BLANDFORD, BROADSTONE, POOLE AND BOURNEMOUTH WEST.**

Left: Having left Manchester at 10am the 'Pines Express' is seen here at Bath Queen Square (Green Park from 1951), whence it will depart as the 2.35pm to Bournemouth West. At its head, and complete with Whitaker's tablet apparatus, is 4-4-0 No 46, built for the Joint Committee in 1928. The photograph is undated but was probably taken *c*1929, judging from the locomotive's S&D livery and a reference to the LMS on the reverse of the print. As Green Park was a terminus the 'Pines' had to reverse at the station. *Ian Allan Library*

Right: The northbound 'Pines Express', double-headed by BR Standard Class 5 4-6-0s Nos 73050 (now preserved) and 73051, passes Henstridge — the smallest station on the line, just south of Templecombe — on 20 May 1958. In the 1950s, with the boom in holidays on the South Coast, the train became ever more popular. *R. Blenkinsop*

Below: A line-up of banking engines in the middle road at Evercreech Junction on a wet 2 August 1958. No fewer than five ex-LMS Class 2P 4-4-0s — Nos 40563, 40568, 40700, 40564 and 40697 — stand ready to assist expresses such as the 'Pines' over the Mendips to Bath. *Ivo Peters*

Left: BR Standard Class 9F 2-10-0 No 92203 thunders over the River Stour at Durweston, one of four crossings of the river by the S&D, with a northbound 'Pines Express' on 31 August 1960. Although never the fastest, this was in its heyday one of the most famous and best-loved cross-country trains in Britain. No 92203 would later be preserved by David Shepherd. *Ian Allan Library*

27

BOURNEMOUTH WEST, TEMPLECOMBE and BATH

Mls. from B'mth W.	Station		Week Days																
			am	am	am	am	am	am	am	am	am	am	am	am	am	am	am		am
	Notes		Mondays to Fridays	Saturdays only				Through Train Bournemouth to Sheffield. Saturdays only. 30th July to 27th August	Through Train Bournemouth to Liverpool. Saturdays only. 16th July to 3rd September			Through Train Bournemouth to Bradford. Saturdays only. 2nd July to 10th September.	Saturdays only	Mondays to Fridays	Mondays to Fridays	Through Train Bournemouth to Liverpool and Manchester. Refreshment Car Bournemouth to Liverpool. Saturdays only	Through Train Bournemouth to Sheffield. Mondays and Fridays only		Refreshment Car Train Bournemouth to Manchester THE PINES EXPRESS. Through Carriages to Liverpool, also Sheffield Tuesdays to Thursdays. Mondays to Fridays
	28 WATERLOO	dep					Y2③40										5Y40		5Y40
	Bournemouth West	dep					6 50	8 0	8 16			8 40	8 48	8 48		9 25	9 30		9 45
1¼	Branksome						6Y36	7Y59	7Y59			8Y33	8 52	8 52		9Y11	9Y 5		9Y 5
2½	Parkstone						6Y40	8 8	8Y 3			8Y37	8 56	8 56		9 36	9Y 9		9Y 9
—	28 Weymouth } Via	dep						6 40	6 40			7 34	7 34	7 34		7 34	7 34		8 25
—	28 Swanage } Poole	,,						7 15	7 15			7 38	7 38	7 38		7 38	7 38		8 58
4½	**Poole**	dep					7 2	8 14	8 24			8 51	9 2	9 2		9 44	9 40		9 54
6½	Creekmoor Halt	,,					6r50	8Y 3	8Y 3			8Y31	9 8	9 8		9Y28	9Y28		9Y28
—	30 Wimborne	dep					6r45	7Y52	7Y52			8r20	8r20	8r20		9Y17	9Y17		9Y17
7¾	Broadstone	dep					7 11	7Y59	7Y59			9 3	9 12	9 12		9Y23	9Y23		9Y23
9½	Corfe Mullen Halt																		
12½	Bailey Gate						7 24						9 23	9 28					
15½	Spetisbury Halt						7 31						9 29	9 35					
17	Charlton Marshal Halt						7 36						9 34	9 40					
18¾	**Blandford Forum**						7 41					9 22	9 40	9 50			10 8		1020
21¼	Stourpaine and Durweston Halt						7 52												
24¼	Shillingstone						7 59						9 51	10 5					
27¼	Sturminster Newton						8 14						9 58	10 13					
31¼	Stalbridge						8 23						10 6	10†19			1031		1038
32¾	Henstridge						8 29						1011						
34½	**Templecombe**	arr					8 40						1021						
—	**31 WATERLOO**	arr					11 8						1 5						
		dep	1 15	1h15											5 40				
—	**Templecombe**	dep	7 0	7 0		8 20				9 10					1020				
38	Wincanton		7 7	7 7		8 28				9 20		9 58			1027				
42¼	Cole		7 16	7 16		8 38				9 29					1036				
45	**Evercreech Junction**	arr	7 23	7 23		8 46		9 22	9 31	9 36		1010			1043	1047	1053		11 1
—	Mls **Evercreech Junction**	dep			8 15						9 55								
—	1½ Pylle				8 20						10 0								
—	5 West Pennard				8 28						10 8								
—	10¼ **Glastonbury and Street**				8 38						1020								
—	13 Ashcott				8 45						1028								
—	15 Shapwick				8 50						1033								
—	17¼ **Edington Burtle**				8 56						1039								
—	21 Bason Bridge				9 4						1046								
—	22¼ **Highbridge and Burnham-on-Sea**	arr			9 8						1051								
—	**Evercreech Junction**	dep	7 24	7 24				9 25	9 35	9 38		1016				1050	1056		11 2
46½	Evercreech New		7 30	7 30						9 45									
49¾	**Shepton Mallet** (Charlton Road)		7 43	7 43						10 1		1033							1118
52¾	Masbury Halt									Q									
54½	Binegar		7 59	7 59						10 17									
57	Chilcompton		8 5	8 5						10 23									
59	Midsomer Norton South		8 10	8 10						10 28									
60¾	**Radstock North**		8 15	8 15						10 33									
63	Shoscombe and Single Hill Halt		8 21	8 21						10 39									
64¾	Wellow		8 25	8 25						10 42									
67¼	Midford		8 31	8 31						10 48									
71½	**Bath Green Park**	arr	8 42	8 42				1023	1031	10 59		1120				1141	1145		1156
—	Bath Green Park	dep	10 1	9 53						12S23						1223			
81¼	Mangotsfield	arr	1022	1015						12S44						1244			
86¼	Bristol (Temple Meads)	,,	1039	1033						1S 3						1 3			
—	Bath Green Park	dep	10G1	9G53				1030	1045			1128				1150	1149		12 1
113½	Gloucester (Eastgate)	arr	1111	1111					1145			1223				1252	1242		1253
120	Cheltenham Spa (Lansdown)	,,	1132	1132				1142	12 7							1 14	1 1		1 12
139¼	Worcester (Shrub Hill)	,,	1233						1 2								2 52		2 52
165¼	Birmingham (New Street)	,,	1243	1243				1 0	1 23			1 56					2 11		2 23
204¾	Leicester (London Road)	,,	2 58	2 58				2 48	2 58			3 45					4 27		4 27
195¼	Burton-on-Trent	,,	1 30	1 30				1 55				2 51					2 55		3T16
206¼	Derby (Midland)	,,	1 45	1 45				2 14				3 7					3 10		3T33
222¼	Nottingham (Midland)	,,	2 41	2 41				3 24				3 44					4 13		4T13
217¾	Crewe	,,	2 18	2 23					2 57							3 47			3 41
248½	Manchester (London Road)	,,	3 30	3 37					4B 0							4 48			4B35
253¼	Liverpool (Lime Street)	,,	4 21	3C54					3 54							4 50			4 50
242½	Sheffield (Midland)	,,	2 47	2 47				3 30				4 16					4 16		4T33
289	York	,,	4 7	4 7				5 35									7 23		7 23
280	Leeds (City)	,,	4 32	4 32								5 37					6 28		6 28
295½	Bradford (Forster Square)	,,	5 8	5 8								6 30					7 9		7 9

G Change at Mangotsfield   r Via Broadstone   Y Via Poole

For other Notes see page 497

For COMPLETE SERVICE between Bournemouth West and Poole, see Table 28—Bournemouth West and Broadstone, Table 30

Extract from Bradshaw's July
5 guide, showing the timings of
northbound 'Pines Express'.

t: The southbound 'Pines
ress' crosses Monkton Combe
duct after leaving the single bore
ombe Down Tunnel. The 12-
ch train, photographed in June
1, is double-headed by ex-MR
0 No 40509 (in its final year)
BR Standard Class 9F 2-10-0
92001. The viaduct, constructed
ue engineering brick, was built to
ommodate double track and
survives. *G. Heiron*

tre right: The up 'Pines Express',
rting a BR alloy headboard, leaves
creech Junction on 18 August
2, double-headed by a pair of BR
ndard locomotives — Class 4MT
0 No 75009 and '9F' 2-10-0
92245; although the '9Fs' were
able of hauling these trains
ssisted the ASLEF union lobbied
etain pilots. This was the final
mer that the 'Pines Express' was
ed over the S&D. *G. Richardson*

ow: Bound for Bournemouth West,
last 'Pines Express' to traverse
S&D roars through Midford behind
aculate Class 9F No 92220
ning Star (now preserved) on
eptember 1962. Immediately
ind the locomotive are two
sley coaches that have been
ed specially for the occasion,
ing this train, at 426 tons, the
viest ever to use the line without a
t. Midford Viaduct survives today
se as a cycleway-cum-footpath.
Allan Library

For many years, until the mid 1950s, the Bath–Bournemouth main line was extremely busy, particularly during peak summer periods, but as travel habits changed, as a result of increasing car ownership, and more freight was transported by road, the fortunes of the line began to decline.

Some closures had already been effected, the Corfe Mullen–Wimborne Junction link closing to passengers in July 1920 and to freight in June 1933. The Burnham–Highbridge line closed to regular passengers in October 1951, at which time the Glastonbury–Wells branch closed to all traffic, while the Edington Junction–Bridgwater line closed to passengers in December 1952 and to all traffic in October 1954. Yet it was considered at the time that the 'takeover' of the line by the Western Region in 1958 was the beginning of the end for the S&D. There had been earlier ill-

feeling between the Western and Southern regions, and once the route was recommended for closure in the Beeching report of 1963 a ruthless run-down, combined with instances of poor management by the Western Region, was considered by many to be deliberate. The 'Pines Express' had been diverted away from the route in 1962, as had the through freight and summer specials that were the line's lifeblood. From 1963 goods facilities at many intermediate stations were withdrawn, and from 1964 the line closed at night. These factors ensured that the remaining local passenger services became increasingly unviable.

Objections to the run-down were to no avail, and closure was finally agreed in September 1965. Plans for economies in running the line were ignored, and a (slower) local bus service was to be introduced once

Left: The first appearance of a three-car DMU at Midsomer Norton South on 10 May 1958. This was a Gloucestershire Railway Society special and one of the very first appearances of a DMU anywhere on the S&D. The signalbox was demolished after closure of the line but has since been rebuilt, and the station is nowadays the focus of the S&D Mendip Main Line Project, which aims to reopen the line towards Chilcompton and Radstock. *Ivo Peters*

Above right: Making for Blandford Forum, the LCGB 'Hampshireman' railtour passes Corfe Mullen Junction on 3 November 1968, after closure of the line to passengers. The train is headed by Class 74 electro-diesel No E6108, on diesel power, assisted at the rear by Class 47 No 1986. *J. Bird*

ie line closed. There were vigorous protests, in particular by railwaymen loyal to the line. A farewell special in January 1966 was brought to a stand at Binegar while the signalman complained about the 'vicious attitude' of BR's Western Region, and staff at Bath refused to sell tickets for the replacement bus service.

Such was the rush for closure that an emergency timetable had to be introduced in January 1966, as proper alternative arrangements had not been made. After 111 years of operation the surviving Highbridge–Evercreech Junction and Bath–Broadstone sections were eventually closed to regular passenger services on 5 March 1966, the final RCTS and SLS specials running the following day. The preceding weeks saw great activity among railway enthusiasts keen to catch a final glimpse of the S&D in action, and in the last days fields, tracks and roads close to the railway were full of photographers keen to record their final memories of this iconic railway.

On some sections freight survived a while longer. Traffic between Bath Junction and Twerton (Bakery Siding) continued until November 1967, and the Broadstone–Blandford section remained open until January 1969. Dairy traffic between Highbridge and Bason Bridge Creamery ceased in October 1972, while the short stretch of line between Radstock and Writhlington Colliery — the final section of the S&D to remain operational — was last used by coal trains in November 1973.

After final closure the track was lifted and the land sold off piecemeal, but many engineering works still exist, including most of the main viaducts and tunnels. Railway walks and cycleways are also a feature of parts of the route, particularly between Bath and Radstock. A number of station buildings also survive, notably Bath Green Park, Midsomer Norton South and Shillingstone.

It is generally accepted that the S&D was a splendid railway, and the line became a particular focus for railway enthusiasts and lovers of the countryside. The S&D was known far more as the 'Swift and Delightful' than the 'Slow and Dirty', but it is generally agreed that it was finally 'Sabotaged and Defeated'. Its surviving traces remain the source of great fascination, and there is, quite rightly, a significant and enduring interest in all things S&D.

Right: Dismantling of the goods crane at Midford goods yard, to the north of the passenger station, on 29 November 1967. Goods facilities had been withdrawn in 1963, and Midford had already become an unstaffed halt by the time the line was closed in 1966. The crude demolition of much of the S&D seemed an ignoble fate for an iconic railway. However, the substantial concrete plinth in the foreground survives, as do the bases of signals and other lineside equipment, and the goods yard, whilst overgrown, was still readily identifiable when the author visited in 2009. *J. Sawtell*

Below right: Midford is a unique location for 'lost' transport. Closed to rail traffic in 1966, the eight-arch, 168yd (153m) S&D viaduct, constructed of blue engineering brick, still survives and is now used as a footpath/cycleway. Some idea of its grand scale is apparent from this photograph, taken on 19 March 2009 and featuring in addition some remnants of the one-time GWR Camerton branch, which passed under the viaduct on its own brick structure (centre). The Somersetshire Coal Canal, which closed in 1898, once passed beneath the northern part of the viaduct, while at the south end of the viaduct can be found the remains of a coal tramway, which closed as long ago as 1874. *Author*

Above: Evercreech Junction on 14 September 1967, with a permanent-way gangers' petrol trolley (No B29W) from Radstock on the centre road, once used by banking locomotives. The sleepers in the demolition gang's wagons are from the (by now) partly lifted Highbridge branch. *J. Vaughan*

Below: Class 33 No 6506 at Bailey Gate station on 4 April 1970, with an engineers' demolition train loaded with lifted track. This was where the Wimborne line once diverged, the two lines running in parallel as far as Corfe Mullen Junction. Bailey Gate signalbox was demolished at this time, but the platforms would survive until 1988. The United Dairies creamery (right), at one time a source of traffic for the railway, has also closed, and today this location is dominated by a road and a roundabout. *J. Bird*

Below: At 1 mile 69yd (1,672m) in length Combe Down Tunnel was the longest unventilated tunnel on the entire BR network. Nowadays sealed, it may (along with Devonshire Tunnel) one day be opened up to cyclists and walkers in this most beautiful rural area. As is apparent from this photograph of the southern portal, taken on 19 March 2009, a considerable quantity of water currently flows out of it, and the steep cutting is stabilised by stone walls. *Author*

Left: Perchance the S&D is not quite dead. The platforms at Shillingstone, seen overgrown in 1995, have since been cleared, and track and trains have returned as part of the Shillingstone Station Project, which aims to restore the station — at one time used by King Edward VII and the poet Rupert Brooke — and recreate the atmosphere of the S&D. Trains have also returned to Midsomer Norton South, and prospects for a modest reawakening of the S&D have never looked brighter. *Author*

7 Weymouth & Portland Joint Railway

The Weymouth & Portland Railway opened in October 1865 as a mixed-gauge line that ran from Weymouth, along Chesil Beach, to Portland. A link to naval installations at Portland was added in 1900. The Easton & Church Hope Railway extended the line to Easton in 1900, and passenger services over the entire 8½-mile branch commenced in September 1902. The two nominally independent but linked railways were operated jointly by the LSWR and GWR from the outset. In 1909 the line ran from a separate station adjoining Weymouth station (to avoid reversing in and out of the busy main line terminal), and this was called

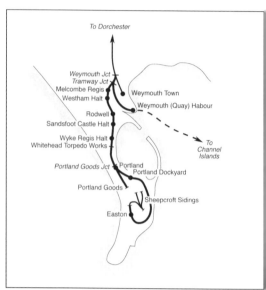

Below: An ex-GWR Class 1366 0-6-0PT, No 1370, still in GWR livery, makes its way bunker-first along the tramway with a freight for Weymouth Quay on 31 May 1950. Note the bell, above the running plate ahead of the cab, for sounding audible warnings when working on the public highway. The maritime nature of this part of Weymouth is readily apparent from the photograph, which includes a ship's chandler and seamen's hostel. *J. Flemons*

Above: Ex-GWR '1366' 0-6-0PT No 1369 is seen having just passed under the Town Bridge with a boat train for Waterloo on 5 August 1961. At this time locomotives would be changed outside the main station at Weymouth Yard for the remainder of the journey to London. No 1369 survives today in preservation on the South Devon Railway. *J. Haydon*

Right: Viewed from the Town Bridge, a standard BR 0-6-0 diesel shunter is seen making its way from Weymouth Quay to Weymouth Yard with an up Channel Islands boat train on 9 June 1968. Even in the 1960s delay has been caused by inconsiderate parking on the congested quayside. A sign beneath the locomotive's front coupling still proclaims the need to keep 50ft clear, and a small bell is mounted above the driver's cab window. *D. Canning*

Melcombe Regis, to reflect the full name of Weymouth.

The broad gauge to Portland was removed in 1874, after virtually no use, the line being worked by the standard-gauge LSWR. Thereafter the line was operated by the GWR and LSWR in alternate years, a situation that continued until 1931, when the SR took over, staff and engineering work being provided by the GWR.

The Portland section provided freight, including the famous Portland building stone, and a number of disused gravity-worked or horse-drawn tramways that once conveyed this stone from the vast quarries can still be found. As passenger traffic grew, platforms were extended, and additional stops provided, the last, at Sandsfoot Castle, opening in 1932. Tourist traffic was not extensive, but naval specials were run in connection with the Portland Naval Base. A siding was added to the torpedo factory at Wyke Regis, and an idea of the area's strategic importance can be gained from the fact that the line suffered air-raid damage during World War 2.

Passenger services were withdrawn in March 1952, and all remaining freight ceased in April 1965, the track being lifted in 1970. The course of the railway was clear to see for many years after closure, and today much of the route to Portland is used as a footpath, the section through Weymouth itself being known as the Rodwell Trail.

The Weymouth & Portland Railway also owned the Weymouth Harbour Tramway. This was originally a horse-worked freight tramway, dating from 1865. It opened to passenger traffic in August 1889 and was worked by the GWR. The mile-long link from the main-line station to the Quay station provided an increasingly important route to and from the Channel Islands, not only for commodities such as potatoes, tomatoes and coal but also for the increasingly busy passenger boat trains. Services developed, and sidings and passing loops were added to serve the harbour businesses and landing stages. Work started on rebuilding the Town Bridge in 1928, and the quay facilities were modernised during the period 1931-3.

Boat trains proceeded through the town's public roads at a 4mph walking pace to meet the Channel Island steamers on the quay itself. Traffic ceased with the German occupation of the Channel Islands in 1940 but recommenced in 1946. In 1959 the decision was made to transfer Channel Island rail traffic from Southampton to Weymouth Quay, following which the tramway prospered and further improvements were made to the quay and its facilities.

The fortunes of the tramway changed in the 1960s reflecting the general decline in rail-borne freight traffic. Freight ceased altogether in 1972, although static oil-tank wagons remained at Weymouth Quay until 1983. In latter years the quayside at Weymouth became notorious for its congestion, and the unique sight of trains running through the busy streets and on the crowded quayside looked increasingly vulnerable. BR's shipping services were privatised in 1984, and in 1987 sailings from Weymouth were withdrawn, regular passenger trains on the tramway ceasing with the final sailings, although the line was last used in May 1999 for a railtour. In 2010 the tramway remains unused as a siding, but not technically closed, while recommenced sailings to the Channel Islands use the facilities at the former Quay railway station.

Left: Hauled by a Class 33/1 fitted with a bell, the boat trtain from Waterloo makes it way towards Weymouth Quay on 23 June 1973. By this time freight traffic had ceased, and even the oil-tank wagons used to refuel the Sealink ferries were left at the terminal as a static installation, being refilled by road tankers. *H. Price*

Left: Consisting of EMU stock hauled by a Class 33, a boat train from Waterloo makes its way along Commercial Road, Weymouth, and towards the Quay station in September 1983. The train is preceded by a pair of flagmen, no warning bell being provided on the locomotive. The use of Class 33/1s in push/pull mode from Bournemouth obviated the need for a locomotive change at Weymouth Yard. *Author*

Below: The start of the tramway section, close to Weymouth's current station, was marked by a gate. This remained in January 2009, when this photograph was taken, together with a rusting connection to the main line, while a colour-light signal still protected the main line from the tramway, a decade after the last train. The tramway still exists, and there are continuing hopes of a revival. *R. Trill*

Below: Unlike the tramway the joint line to Portland required numerous bridges and even a short tunnel near Rodwell. This photograph, taken near Rodwell in January 2009, shows the disused trackbed which nowadays forms the basis of the well-used Rodwell Trail through the southern outskirts of Weymouth and leading to the Isle of Portland. *R. Trill*

⑧ Severn & Wye Joint Railway

The beauty of the Forest of Dean today belies the fact that two centuries ago the area was at the forefront of the Industrial Revolution. As long ago as 1810 the Severn & Wye Railway & Canal Co opened a tramway that served the mineral deposits, particularly iron and coal in the forest, and linked them to the canal. The lines were built to a gauge of about 3ft 6in (later widened to 3ft 8in) and were worked with private wagons and horses. A complex network of lines soon developed, largely as a result of the area's diverse geology, and by 1813 encompassed about 30 miles of tramway.

The growth of mineral traffic led to steam locomotives' being introduced in 1864, and in 1869 some 8 miles were converted to broad gauge to link with the GWR at Lydney Junction. However, in 1872 this section and most of the rest of the network was converted to standard gauge, becoming known as the Severn & Wye Railway, which in 1879 merged with the Severn Bridge Railway to become the Severn & Wye & Severn Bridge Joint Railway.

The key engineering feature on the joint railway was the graceful Severn Bridge, which opened in October 1879 and connected the GWR at Lydney with the

BERKELEY ROAD, LYDNEY, and LYDBROOK (1st and 3rd class).—Great Western and Midland Joint.
Traffic Man., John A. Carter, Lydney.

[Timetable — Week Days]

‡ Station for Staunton. § Troy Station. ‖ Great Western Station. ¶ High Street Station. ** May Hill Station. ‡‡ Temple Meads.

Notes:
a Thursdays and Saturdays.
b Wednesdays only.
c Runs from Berkeley on notice being given to the Station Master not later than 2 aft.
d Stops when required on information being given to the Guard.
g Mondays, Tuesdays, & Thursdays.
h Runs forward to Berkeley on notice being given to the Guard.
* Station for Blakeney.
† Station for Clearwell.

The diagram shows a railway map with the following labels:

To Ross-on-Wye · To Ross-on-Wye · Grange Court · Lydbrook Jct · Lower Lydbrook Halt · Upper Lydbrook · Symond's Yat · To Monmouth · Waterloo Col · Drybrook Road · Drybrook Jct · Churchway · Laymoor Jct · Bilson Goods · Cinderford · Bilson Jct · WillmseyJct · Serridge Jct · Foxes Bridge Col · Wimberry Quarry · Wimberry Jct · Speech House Road · Purples Hill Quarry · To Monmouth · Coleford · Woodgreens Col · Biscade Quarry · Lightmoor Col · Biscade Jct · New Fancy Col · Easter Iron Ore Mining · Milkwall · Point Quarry · Coleford Jct · New Ham Pit · Futterhill Sidings · Parkend · Van Siding · Parkend Goods · Parkend Jct · Phipps Siding · Whitecroft · Tufts North Jct · Princess Royal Sidings · Severn Bridge · Severn Bridge · RIVER SEVERN · Tufts South Jct · Norchard Col · Kidnall's Col · Middle Forge · Lydney Town · N Docks Branch or Sharpness Jct · Sharpness · Gloucester & Berkeley Ship Canal · Calour Works Siding · Lydney Jct · Engine Shed Jct · Sharpness Docks Goods · Whimsey · To Gloucester · Lydney · Lydney Jct · Oldminster Jct · Lydney Harbour · Berkeley · Berkeley Road Jct · Berkeley Road · G.W.R. · Docks Jct · Berkeley Loop Jct · SEVERN ESTUARY · Berkeley Road South Jct · To Newport · To Bristol

DEAN FOREST RAILWAY
LYDNEY—PARKEND

Below left: Berkeley Road–Lydbrook service as listed in the April 1910 *Bradshaw's Guide*. Note the spelling of 'Berkeley' in the title.

Bottom left: An auto-train from Berkeley Road, comprising ex-GWR 14xx' 0-4-2T No 1444 (fitted with push-pull apparatus for railmotor work) and compartment railmotor coach No W250W, after arrival at Sharpness one evening in August 1964. The line had been reduced to single track in 1956, and steps that ran from the unused island platform to the road between the two bridge arches have been removed, as has the locomotive's front numberplate. *A. Muckley*

Below: Passenger services on the remaining Berkeley Road–Sharpness section were withdrawn in November 1964, and this photograph shows Sharpness station shortly after closure. The object in the foreground (right) is the base of the metal water tower, which has been cut up for scrap. *S. Allen*

Midland Railway at Berkeley Road. However the opening, by the GWR in 1886, of the Severn Tunnel resulted in a reduction in traffic using the bridge, adversely affecting the financial position of the joint railway, and in 1894 the latter was rescued by the GWR and MR, becoming the Great Western & Midland Severn & Wye Joint Railway. The new owners created a joint managing committee; this provided much-needed capital for stock and a new line into Cinderford, but equally the committee remitted funds to the Midland and Great Western railways.

Following the Grouping the LMS sometimes reversed the title of the joint railway — LMS&GWR S&W — reflecting the fact that the LMS was the largest of the 'Big Four' companies. The network at that time comprised about 40 miles of line, and motive power was provided by both partners.

While the area's natural resources contributed substantial freight traffic, a passenger service was also provided. At its peak this included eight trains in each direction, serving most stations, along with additional trains over the Severn Bridge. However, most settlements were small, and the only passenger services to survive after July 1929 were those over the Severn Bridge between Lydney Town and Berkeley Road.

During World War 2 the Forest of Dean was used to store ammunition, and a military depot at Corn Patch despatched 80 wagons a day. After the war traffic declined, and as collieries and ironworks in the forest closed the railways contracted. In January 1956 the Upper Lydbrook–Mierystock Siding section was closed, severing the northern outlet for forest traffic and in November 1960 the ex-S&W lines north of Speech House Road followed suit. August 1963 witnessed the closure of the link to Lydney Docks, the last section of the mineral loop ceased operation in June 1964, and the NCB shut down its sole remaining colliery in 1965. The lines north of Parkend closed in August 1967, leaving the stretch south to Lydney Junction as the final section of line to retain a freight service, until May 1976; thereafter the track remained in situ pending a resumption of regular traffic, but in July 1981 the Parkend line was officially declared closed.

An important diversionary route used as an alternative to the Severn Tunnel, the Severn Bridge was severed by a barge in October 1960 and damaged again in 1961, whereupon the decision was taken not to repair the structure, and through services were formally withdrawn. However, passenger trains on the remaining Berkeley Road–Sharpness stub continued until November 1964, and this section remains open today for freight.

In the Forest of Dean much of the former trackbed is now used as footpaths, although Lydbrook Viaduct was demolished in 1970, and some tunnels have been sealed. However, in 1995 the Lydney Junction–Parkend section was reopened throughout by the preserved Dean Forest Railway.

Left: Once the decision was taken to phase out loose-coupled four-wheeled wagons on BR these were sometimes left to rot for years before being scrapped. This view of a rusting wagon was recorded at disused dock sidings at Sharpness in June 1993. *Author*

Below: The unique semaphore signal — red with a white circle — used to control rail and road traffic over the South Dock swing bridge at Sharpness, pictured in June 1993. Both bridge and signal have since been dismantled. *Author*

Above: Traffic over the huge yet elegant Severn Bridge ceased abruptly in October 1960 when the bridge pier was struck and line severed by the tanker barge *Wastdale H.* This view from the Lydney shore, showing the loss of one pier and both adjoining spans, was recorded on 18 April 1964 and also features a 2-8-0 heading a northbound freight on the ex-GWR line to Gloucester. The bridge was allowed to deteriorate after the accident and was later demolished. *B. Ashworth*

Right: In charge of the 11.52am Berkeley Road–Lydney Town auto-train, ex-GWR '14xx' 0-4-2T No 1401 (which, incidentally, was used in the filming of *The Titfield Thunderbolt*) takes water at Lydney Junction before proceeding to its destination. This would be the last section of the S&W in the Dean Forest to retain its passenger services, until October 1960. The station is now part of the preserved Dean Forest Railway. *R. Toop*

Right: Parkend station on 8 April 1989, no longer the spick-and-span site it had been in the pre-World War 1 era and as yet still out of use, awaiting restoration by the Dean Forest Railway. The level crossing would be reinstated, replica S&W station buildings installed and passenger services restored in 2006, after an interval of some 77 years. *R. Ruffell*

Above: The mineral wealth of the area continued to provide freight for the railways. Ex-GWR '57xx' 0-6-0PT No 3737 is pictured arriving at Coleford Junction, north of Parkend, with a train of empty hoppers for the stone quarries at Whitecliff on 2 July 1964. Coleford wagons were detached from Cinderford services in the goods yard here. *Ian Allan Library*

Left: The distinctive stone portal of the 242yd (221m) Mierystock Tunnel on the lifted Lydbrook Junction–Serridge Junction section, seen in August 1966, a decade after it was last used. The tunnel has since been sealed and a detour provided for the walkway/cycleway that now uses the old railway trackbed here.
B. Quemby

Left: The end of the line at Lydney Docks was marked by a wagon turntable, the remains of which are seen here on 27 March 2009. The turntable allowed coal and iron-ore wagons to be manœuvred onto a hoist and into ships below. Most coal was destined for ports between Bristol and Ilfracombe. The outer dock basin was completed in 1821. The last commercial vessel used the dock in October 1960, and the railway closed in August 1963. The entire length of the dock branch is now used as a footpath. *Author*

Wales and the Marches

Right: A ballast train headed by an unidentified 0-6-0PT approaches Rhydycar Junction, near Merthyr Tydfil, from the Vaynor limestone quarries before closure of this last remaining section of the ex-B&M & LNW Joint Railway in November 1967. *R. Hancock*

Surprisingly, in view of the complex network of lines that developed in the South Wales Coalfield area, there were comparatively few joint railways in Wales, but this was perhaps because of the ultimately extensive network of the GWR and the heavy volumes of coal freight. However, several joint lines were established as a result of the LNWR's incursion into South Wales. The GWR also had a couple of joint ventures with the Rhymney Railway, while the GWR and LNWR came together with a number of joint lines in the Welsh Marches.

LNW joint railways in South Wales
The Brecon & Merthyr & LNW Joint was the largest of three joint ventures involving the LNWR in South Wales, which from 1875 provided the LNWR with a link from Abergavenny, via its Heads of the Valleys line, to Merthyr Tydfil. This area was remote from the LNWR's main depots, so while the LNWR put pressure on the B&MR to share its 6-mile line into Merthyr, the B&MR recovered half the costs of construction from the LNWR.

Two other short but strategically important joint railways were also operated in association with the Heads of the Valleys line. First was the Nantybwch & Rhymney Joint Railway, a 3-mile LNW/Rhymney joint line which from September 1867 provided a link to Rhymney. Second was the Brynmawr & Western

Valleys line, a short (1¼-mile) GW/LNW joint line that opened to all traffic in May 1906 and ran, as its title suggested, from Brynmawr to Nantyglo, where connection with the GWR provided links to Newport and the Western Valleys.

All the lines remained in joint LMS/GWR ownership from 1923 until 1948. The Heads of the Valleys line closed in January 1958, although trains ran to Nantybwch until 1960, and freight traffic over the Merthyr–Vaynor Quarry line, part of the ex-B&M & LNW Joint, continued until August 1966.

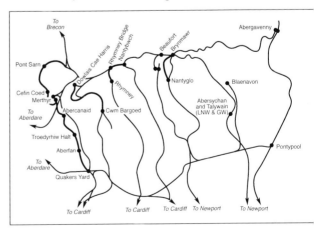

43

Left: Cefn Coed Viaduct on the former B&M & LNW Joint Railway, pictured on 21 July 2008. Built on a graceful curve, this elegant stone structure, with its 15 arches, is 725ft (220m) long and rises 122ft (37m) above the Taff Fawr. Its construction led to the bankruptcy of contractor Thomas Savin in 1866 but provided the LNWR with a grand entry to Merthyr Tydfil. *Author*

Above: LNW & Rhymney Railways Joint Lines cast-iron sign at Rhymney station. The short joint line connecting with the Heads of the Valleys route gave the LNWR access over the RR to Cardiff Docks and the LNWR warehouse at Tyndall Street. *P. Ransome-Wallis*

GW & Rhymney joint railways in South Wales

Opened in 1876 the Taff Bargoed Railway, linking Llancaiach Junction with Dowlais Cae Harris, was a GW & Rhymney line, its construction being a joint venture. Much of the line passed through a sparse and wild valley, but passenger services survived until 1964. Freight to the steelworks at Dowlais continued longer, until 1983, and as recently as 2006 the rusting track could still be seen on the southern part of the route. Track just north of Cwm Bargoed, including the zig-zag lines at Dowlais, has all been removed, but the line to Cwm Bargoed has been reopened for opencast coal workings.

The Merthyr & Quakers Yard Joint line was also a GW & Rhymney joint railway. It ran, as its title suggests, from Quakers Yard, on the GWR Vale of Neath line, up the western side of the Vale of Merthyr to Rhydycar Junction, near Merthyr Tydfil — a distance of 6½ miles. Opened in 1886 and absorbed by the GWR in 1923, it duplicated much of the Taff Vale line on the other side of the valley and closed to passengers in February 1951. The line once served Aberfan, scene of the tragedy of October 1966 in which a rain-sodden mountain of coal waste engulfed the local school, with devastating loss of life. The viaduct at Quakers Yard was blown up in 1969, having been rendered unsafe by mining subsidence. Much of the trackbed is today used as part of the Taff Vale Trail, a long-distance footpath from Cardiff to Brecon, while mining activity has ended and the slag heaps are gone.

Left: The Taff Bargoed Railway was a GW & Rhymney joint venture that provided an important link to Dowlais Iron Works. Here ex-GWR '56xx' 0-6-2T No 5634 is seen at Dowlais Cae Harris with the 1.55pm to Ystrad Mynach, on 24 November 1962. The passenger service was withdrawn in June 1964, and all freight traffic here had ceased by 1983. *L. Sandler*

Right: The stone-built three-road locomotive shed at Dowlais Cae Harris, seen from the station in May 1964. Coded as a sub-shed of Merthyr (88D), it closed in December 1964 but was not demolished until 1981. The despoiled industrial landscape of the time is readily apparent in this view. *R. Holmes*

Right: The 'Cross-Country' DMU used for the Warwickshire Railway Society's 'South Wales Valley Tour' of 13 April 1968 pauses at Cwm Bargoed, on the one-time Taff Bargoed joint line. This location was some 1,250ft above sea level, requiring gradients as steep as 1 in 35 near Cwm Bargoed. Following a period of closure the line south of Cwm Bargoed was reopened in 2008 for coal traffic. *R. Toop*

Below: GW & Rhymney Joint Line timetable, April 1910.

CARDIFF, DOWLAIS, and MERTHYR (1st and 3rd class).—Great Western and Rhymney.

Miles	Up. Rhymney Station,	mrn	mrn	aft	K	aft	aft	K	aft	aft	aft	aft	mrn	aft	Notes
	Cardiff ....dep.	9 15	10 50		2 10	3	5 4	4 30	5 27	6 5 8	10 9 40	11 0	9 0	5 5	a Motor Car, one class only.
3¼	Llanishen	9 22	10 58		2 16	3 13	5 35	6 13	8 13	8 9 47		11 7	9 7	5 12	K Via Hengoed Junction.
7	Caerphilly 67	9 31	11 6		2 25	3 21	4 43	5 42	6 21	8 26 9 55		11 15	9 15	5 20	s Saturdays only.
9¼	Llanbradach	9 38	11 13		2 31	3 27	5 48	6 27	8 32	10 1		11 22	9 21	5 26	¶ "Halt" at Troedyrhiw between Aberfan & Abercanaid.
12¼	Ystrad Mynach ....[71	9 45	11 21		2 37	3 34	4 53	5 54	6 33	8 42	10 8	11 36	9 27	5 32	
14¼	Llancaiach Junc. 70,	9 50	11 43		2 53	3 40	4 59	6 17	18 46	10 13		11 41	9 32	5 37	
—	Llancaiach Jn. dep.	9 58		1 0	3 13		5 13		7 20	8s50	1033				
18¾	Bedlinog	10 7		1 9	3 22		5 22		7 29	8s59	1042				
21½	Cwm Bargoed ..[464	1015		1 17	3 30		5 30		7 37	9 s 7	1050				
24¼	Dowlais (Cae Harris)	1025		1 27	3 40		5 40		7 47	9s17	11 0				
16	Treharris ......[109	9 57	11 48		2 59	3 44	5 4	6 6	7 7	8 52	10 19	1147	9 43	5 48	
17	Quaker's Yard 70,108	10 1	11 52		3a14	3 47	5 7	6 9	7a25	8 8 55	10 23	1150	9 51	5 56	
19½	Aberfan, for Merthyr	10 6	11 57		3a20	3 52	5 12	6 15	7a25 9	1 10 28		1155	9 57	6 2	
22¼	Abercanaid ¶ ....[Vale	1013	12 5		3a28	4 0	5 19		7a35 9	8 10 34					
24	Merthyr 67, 464 arr.	1019	12 12		3a35	4 5	5 25	6 25	7a40 9	14 10 40		12 5	10 7	6 12	

☞ **Other Trains**

BETWEEN
Cardiff & Ystrad Mynach 470

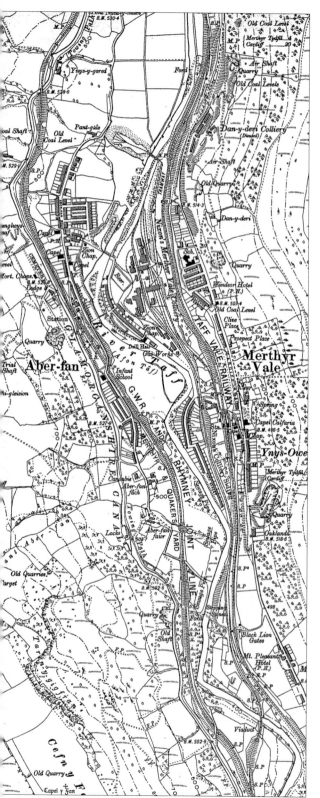

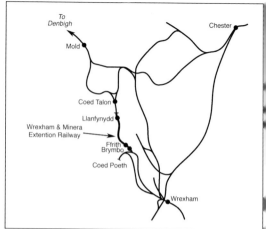

Wrexham & Minera Extension Railway

The only joint railway in North Wales was opened in January 1872 and operated a 3-mile line linking the GWR and LNWR. It retained its title in 1923, surrendering its joint status only in 1948. The two intermediate joint stations were served by Mold–Brymbo passenger trains, which ceased to run in March 1950, and the line closed completely in January 1972.

The Welsh Marches

The Shrewsbury–Buttington line became a joint GW/LNW operation in 1865, while joint working of the Shrewsbury–Hereford line followed in 1875, both lines providing links to and from Wales and within the Welsh borderlands. They remained in joint GWR/LMS ownership after 1923, and the main lines are still open today, but they have lost status, and all but three intermediate stations (of an original total of more than 30) have been closed.

The three ex-GW/LNW joint branches have fared less well. The 4½-mile branch from Cruckmeole Junction to Minsterley, opened in February 1861, closed to passengers in February 1951 and entirely in May 1967. The Ludlow–Bitterley branch, almost six miles in length, opened in August 1864, never had a regular passenger service, but at Clee Hill a cable-worked incline served a granite quarry; this closed in November 1960, and the branch itself in October 1962. The 5-mile Woofferton–Tenbury Wells branch, opened in August 1861, closed to passengers and freight in July 1961, but freight trains continued to run to Tenbury Wells on the ex-GWR (only) line from Bewdley until April 1965.

Left: The GW & Rhymney joint line at Aberfan in 1901. From left to right are shown the Glamorganshire Canal (closed here by 1942), the joint line (closed 1951), the River Taff and the ex-Taff Vale Railway, which is the only line on this map still to remain open. *Crown copyright*

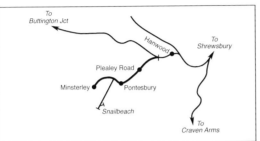

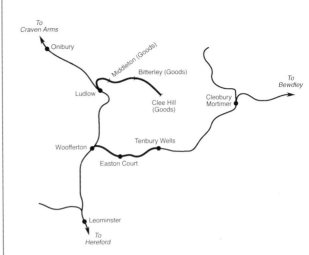

Top: Aberfan was on the Merthyr & Quaker's Yard line, a GW & Rhymney joint operation. The sign, photographed in July 2008, belongs to perhaps the saddest Station Hill in the world, which now leads not to Aberfan station but to the graves of 116 children killed by the heap of coal slag which engulfed the village school in October 1966. *Author*

Above right: The Clee Hill (or Bitterley) joint LNW/GW freight-only branch was linked to two steeply graded quarry mineral lines. This view, over the top of the incline at Clee Hill, shows an empty cable-hauled wagon on its way up and was recorded on 14 May 1956. Note the joint use of the central rail on the incline, which survived until 1962. *Hugh Davis*

Right: The Minsterley branch was a joint LNW/GW line. Here, on 14 June 1958, ex-GWR '57xx' 0-6-0PT No 9657 is seen shunting at Plealey Road, one of two intermediate stations on the branch. At Pontesbury the branch once made a connection with the Snailbeach narrow-gauge railway, serving lead mines in the area. *Hugh Davis*

Right: Tenbury Wells station in March 1961. The individualistic design of the ex-Tenbury Railway station and signalbox are worthy of note. A GWR line ran east from the station to join the Severn Valley Railway at Bewdley, and ex-GWR diesel railcars provided many of the passenger services in the line's latter days. Closure came in 1965. *D. Lawrence*

10 Surburban London

Used intensively by commuters, most of the formerly joint railways in Central London remain open. An exception is the mile-long branch from South Acton to Hammersmith & Chiswick, which opened in 1858 as part of the North & South Western Junction Railway — a joint venture by the London & North Western, Midland and North London railways. Passenger services ceased in January 1917, and the branch closed entirely in May 1965.

In suburbia there have been more closures. Victorian London was expanded by the railways, and once a railway was built suburban development usually followed. To the north of London the

Metropolitan Railway had great plans for the extension of London suburbs into what became known as 'Metro-Land'. The opening of the GCR's 'London Extension' brought main-line trains to the 'Met', and as the two railways had the same chairman a merger was considered. Agreement was eventually reached in 1906 whereby the Met, whilst retaining ownership of its lines and continuing to run its own trains, leased lines north of Harrow-on-the-Hill to the Metropolitan & Great Central Joint Committee, while freight operations were undertaken by each company over alternate five-year periods.

The northern extremity of the Joint Committee's influence was Verney Junction, just over 50 miles from Baker Street in Central London and served by a branch from Quainton Road. Verney was named after a local landowner, and a small railway settlement with distinctive steep-hipped roofs and a hotel grew up around the remote junction. As it turned out 'Metro-Land' never developed along the branch line, and the area has remained rural. Consequently passenger services between Quainton Road and Verney Junction were withdrawn in July 1936, although freight continued until 1956.

In 1926 management of the line passed to the Met, which in 1933 was absorbed by London Transport, but the line continued to be known as the MetGC until BR days. Although Verney Junction station has been demolished, much of the alignment south to Quainton Road is still discernible amid the rolling Buckinghamshire landscape, even though most bridges have been removed since closure of the line.

Left: Verney Junction in prewar days, with the station nameboard framed by the cab and tender of ex-LNWR 'Cauliflower' 0-6-0 No 8535. The station was 50½ miles from Baker Street and was the furthest from London on the MetGC. Although an interchange for Oxford, Cambridge and Banbury, the MetGC line to Quainton Road was not a success and closed to passengers in 1936. Freight lasted longer, until 1956. *D. Hyson*

Right: Departures from Verney Junction *c*1933.

Quainton Road station also closed to regular passenger trains in 1936, but the situation here is rather different from that at Verney Junction inasmuch as the station survives and is now used by the Buckinghamshire Railway Society. There is also the ex-MetGC Brill Tramway Walk, which follows much of the former tramway from Quainton Road to Brill (the history of which is related in *Lost Lines: London*).

To the south of London, the Tooting, Merton & Wimbledon Railway opened in October 1868. Owned jointly by the LBSCR and LSWR (which two companies also collaborated in running the Southsea branch, closed in 1914), this operated two somewhat duplicating loop lines between Wimbledon and Tooting. The 2-mile southerly route through Merton Abbey closed to passengers in March 1929. Freight survived longer, the Tooting–Merton Abbey section finally closing in August 1968, and that between Merton Park and Merton Abbey in May 1975.

Elsewhere in South London was the 2½-mile Woodside & South Croydon Railway, originally a joint SER/LBSCR line, closed in May 1983 (and described more fully in *Lost Lines: London*). Much of its length is now used by Croydon Tramlink.

Below: Verney Junction was named after a local landowner associated with the building of the railway. In 2010 it remains a small Buckinghamshire hamlet, with no station, yet it retains its name, as this road sign, photographed in September 2007, shows. *Author*

Above left: A lineside crossing sign at Verney Junction, photographed in September 2007. A platform edge could just be discerned, deep within a mass of young trees, this section of the Oxford– Cambridge route having closed in 1993. The overgrown track remains *in situ* and has since been cleared in part, as there are plans to reopen this line, albeit not the station or the link to Quainton Road. *Author*

Below: Although most former joint lines in the London area remain open a number of intermediate stations and halts have closed. The derelict up station building at Haddenham, on the ex-GW & GC joint line, is seen here on 22 December 1974. The original station closed in January 1963, but a new station was provided in 1987, and the line here has since been restored to double track. *Ian Allan Library*

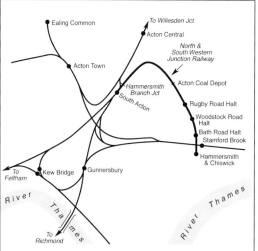

Above: Ex-LSWR Adams Class O2 0-4-4T No 30199 at Hammersmith & Chiswick station with a Railway Enthusiasts' Club tour on 25 March 1962. Although 'O2s' were used on the Isle of Wight until 1966, this was one of the last on mainland Britain. Never electrified, this line from Acton, with three intermediate halts, was the only branch of the jointly operated North & South Western Junction Railway to close completely, in May 1965. *L. Sandler*

Below: Although the branch was single-track, the sidings of the station yard at Hammersmith & Chiswick required a substantial bridge under the current District Line, near Stamford Brook station. Used nowadays by a footpath and for car parking, it is one of very few physical remains of the joint branch and is seen here on Friday 13 March 2009. *Author*

Above: The disused platforms for Merton Abbey at Merton Park, on the LBSCR/LSWR joint line. The Merton Park–Tooting section was never electrified, passenger services being withdrawn in March 1929, and all remaining freight ceased in May 1975. The buildings seen here can still be found in private occupation, just off the route of Croydon Tramlink. *J. Scrace*

Left: The Woodside Junction–Selsdon Junction link of the former Woodside & South Croydon Railway was one of the few sections of electrified third-rail route in London to close, on Friday 13 May 1983. This photograph, taken in September 1997, shows the remains of a porcelain insulator on the trackbed. Most of the route is now used by Croydon Tramlink, and parts of the old line have been reduced to street level. *Author*

Below: Bingham Road Halt, seen still with a SR nameboard on 31 January 1978. The first halt at this location, on the Woodside & South Croydon Railway, had opened in 1906 and closed in 1915 only to be reopened by the SR in 1935; it closed again in May 1983 and was demolished apart from a few scant remains. *J. Glover*

11 Midland & Great Northern Joint Railway

The M&GN provided a wonderful cross-country route extending from the Midlands, through the Lincolnshire Fens, to Norwich and the Norfolk coast. With its handsome golden-ochre locomotives, somersault signals and long sections of single track it was a distinctive and well-known operation and became the most extensive joint railway, with 183¾ miles of line.

The M&GN has a complex history, having been formed largely by the amalgamation of smaller railways rather than conceived from the outset as a trunk route. The first section of what would ultimately become the M&GN was the Spalding–Holbeach line, opened in 1858 by the Norwich and Spalding Railway. This was followed by the amalgamation locally of other, smaller railway companies, forming, in the west, the Midland & Eastern Railway and, in the east, the Eastern & Midlands Railway. However, the latter's financial difficulties led to a takeover in 1893 by the Midland and Great Northern railways, which established the jointly owned M&GN, with its administrative headquarters in King's Lynn. The last 'pure' M&GN section completed, in 1906, was a short section at Runton East Junction, concluding almost half a century of railway construction.

The Joint Committee established was similar in arrangement to the S&D, while chairmanship alternated between the GNR and MR. The M&GN had no official chairman in overall charge but nevertheless constituted a separate railway company, with its own seal and crest, enabling it to own property, undertake

legal proceedings and generally act as other railway companies.

Whilst not encountering any difficult geographical terrain, the line passed through a 330yd (302m) tunnel to the west of Bourne. Its fenland section also crossed the navigable River Nene, by the Cross Keys swing bridge, at Sutton Bridge and the River Ouse near South

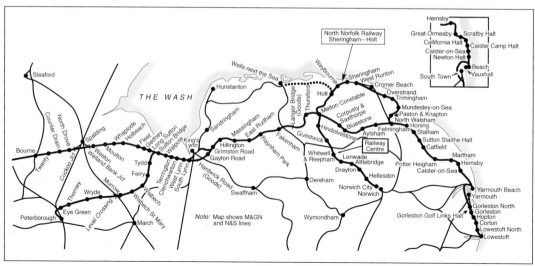

Below left: M&GN garter crest, including coats-of-arms from towns along the route — (clockwise from top left) Peterborough, Norwich, Great Yarmouth and King's Lynn.

Right: North Walsham, with Beyer Peacock 4-4-0 No 23, delivered in 1882, in charge of a goods train. The Eastern & Midlands Railway signals were replaced by M&GN somersault signals after the Joint Committee took over in 1893, giving a clue to the date. This view, which provides an essence of the railway, was used as a basis for the Station Inn pub sign at Holbeach. *Ian Allan Library*

Centre right: 4-4-2T No 41, built at Melton Constable in 1904, seen at Great Yarmouth Beach station in the M&GN's striking golden-ochre livery. The wonderful character of the railway is apparent from this pre-World War 1 view. Neither the station nor the buildings seen in the background survive. *Ian Allan Library*

Below: On loan to the M&GN, ex-MR 4-4-0 No 785 passes South Lynn West signalbox with a Yarmouth–Nottingham train on 30 June 1936. Note the automatic tablet-exchanger on the tender. South Lynn had been used for freight since 1864, but in 1885 the passenger station was completed, avoiding the need to use the GER station in the town. South Lynn station closed to passengers in February 1959, while the coal yard closed in May 1966. *H. C. Casserley*

Lynn, by the five-span Clenchwarton girder bridge. Both bridges were subject to weight restrictions, which limited for all time the motive power that could be used over the line.

Agricultural produce was the main freight traffic generated in the area, although fish trains were once a feature of the line. Summer passengers to the Norfolk coast severely tested the system, which had over 100 miles of single track and numerous speed restrictions; indeed, so heavy was the use of the railway at peak holiday periods that excursion trains even ran during the night. Pride of the line were the 'Leicesters', working to and from the Midlands.

The 1923 Grouping initially resulted in little change for the M&GN, which was now run by the LMS and LNER. In 1936, however, the latter assumed sole responsibility and, as time progressed, increasingly provided its own motive power (albeit still limited by weight restrictions) to take over from the M&GN's veteran locomotives, while administration of the line was transferred from King's Lynn to Liverpool Street.

In 1948 the M&GN became just another BR line, part of the Eastern Region. Decline soon quickened pace; the long cross-country route was vulnerable to road competition, which increasingly captured both agricultural and summer passenger traffic, while the ex-GER lines duplicated many of the destinations. There were also numerous level crossings, while

repairs to Clenchwarton Bridge at South Lynn were required and considered prohibitive. Consequently the M&GN fell victim to the first large-scale railway closure in Britain, all but 15 miles of line closing to passengers completely with effect from 28 February 1959.

A number of short lengths were retained in order to honour existing freight contracts, for even in the late 1950s many local goods services were still being provided; indeed, new links were added at Murrow and near Reepham to allow short sections to remain open for freight use. The Cromer Beach–Melton Constable section was also retained initially for passenger and freight use, but the Sheringham–Melton Constable section closed in 1964, and the remaining freight sections had all succumbed by June 1983, leaving the 3¾-mile stub between Sheringham and Cromer Beach as the last section of the M&GN to remain open as part of the national network.

There was still pride in the line at the end, and on the last day of service in 1959 well-maintained stations could be found throughout the system. Little had really been done to secure economies or to keep the line abreast of the times; somersault signals survived until the end, and many sections never even saw a DMU.

Since closure several stretches of the M&GN have been turned into footpaths or roads, while the Sheringham–Holt section has been reopened as the North Norfolk Railway.

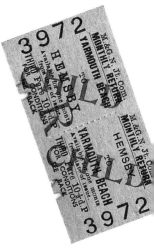

Left: M&GN 0-6-0 No 86, a standard GNR type with a Melton stovepipe chimney fitted. These locomotives were generally used on goods services on the western section of the line, this example being seen near Thursford, on 4 July 1936. *Ian Allan Library*

Right: Ex-M&GN 0-6-0 No 58, at Great Yarmouth Beach station on 28 May 1937. Dating from 1896, the locomotive was built by Neilson to the standard MR Johnson goods design. The '0' number prefix was added by the LNER. Note the somersault shunting signal, with the signal arm higher up the post than the lamp. *H. C. Casserley*

Right: Exchanging the tablet at speed at Massingham on 16 April 1947. The tablet-exchanger, designed by Alfred Whitaker and used in conjunction with the apparatus on the tender, can be seen between the signalbox and the line. The apparatus allowed single-line exchanges at speed and was adopted on the M&GN from 1906. Forty-two complete exchangers were installed, together with 25 receivers or deliverers, on more than 100 miles of single line. *H. C. Casserley*

Right: North Walsham station, photographed on 2 April 1953 from the footbridge seen previously. Ivatt Class 4MT 2-6-0 No 43159, delivered new to the line, waits at the signals (replaced since the earlier view) for the single line as Class B12/3 4-6-0 No 61520 arrives from Melton Constable. The station was demolished after closure. *H. James*

Above: Ivatt Class 4 2-6-0 No 43104 leaving West Lynn Bridge (also known as Clenchwarton Bridge) and crossing the River Ouse with a local train to Peterborough in June 1952. The single-track bridge had five metal lattice-girder spans, of which the three central spans were each 117ft (36m) long, the outer two 70ft (21m). The need for repair work on this bridge was a key factor in deciding to close the line, yet in 2010 the four sets of metal supporting peirs remain perfectly true and intact. *P. Ransome-Wallis*

Above left: Ivatt Class 4 2-6-0 No 43086 coming off the single-line Cross Keys bridge over the River Nene at Sutton Bridge with a train to Peterborough North on 9 August 1958; branching off in the foreground (right) is the station-avoiding line. Operated hydraulically from a nearby engine room (see *Lost Lines: Eastern*), the bridge opened in 1897 and carried both road and rail on a steel swing section some 176ft (54m) long. It remains in use but today carries two lanes of road traffic. *F. Church*

Left: The same train standing at the island platform at Sutton Bridge station on 9 August 1958. From 1866 Sutton Bridge became the junction for the Wisbech line. The station area was last used for freight in May 1965, and after a period of dereliction the railway buildings were demolished. *F. Church*

Above: As the GNR looked after civil engineering on 'The Joint', as it was affectionately known, almost all of the line was eventually operated by GNR-style somersault signals. Taken at Norwich City in the 1950s, this photograph shows a typically tall signal with a somersault arm on a concrete post, which would have been fabricated at Melton Works, but the shunting signal (indicated by an 'S') is of the standard upper-quadrant variety. *A. Wright*

Above right: Ex-LMS Class 4F 0-6-0 No 44122 heads the afternoon through train (with coaches from Birmingham and Leicester to Cromer, Norwich and Yarmouth) at Holbeach station, 9 August 1958. The brick building on the right remains in 2010, having for a time been threatened with the same fate as befell the wooden structures on the left, which have long since been demolished. *F. Church*

Right: On 13 June 1957 ex-LNER Class J39 0-6-0 No 64968 stands at Whitwell & Reepham station with the 3.35pm Class J freight from Norwich City, about to be passed by the 4.30pm from Melton Constable, hauled by ex-GER Class D16/3 4-4-0 No 62515. Not well sited for the settlements it served, the station escaped demolition after final closure of the line in 1983 and is now the focus of a preservation project. *E. Tuddenham*

12 The Crewe of North Norfolk

Remote fields in north Norfolk seem an unlikely location to choose for a railway works, yet such was the case at Melton Constable. A small and isolated village, this was destined to become the most important junction on the entire M&GN network. The first line at Melton Constable, from Fakenham, opened officially in January 1882, while the Melton Constable–Norwich line had opened in full by December of that year. The North Walsham line followed in April 1883, providing a link to Yarmouth, while that to Holt was opened in October 1884 and by 1887 had been extended to Sheringham and Cromer.

From the outset a locomotive shed and workshop was established, and as the network of lines developed Melton Constable became both its engineering centre, with its own foundry and erecting shop, and a busy junction — so much so that it became known as the 'Crewe of North Norfolk'. Neat rows of railway workers' cottages were built to a distinct design, and joining these were a shop, pub, school, church and gasworks, providing the atmosphere of an industrial town in the heart of rural Norfolk.

The M&GN was a self-contained railway, and between 1897 and 1909 nine tank engines were built at the works. Locomotive rebuilding was also undertaken, the work including fitting distinctive 'Melton chimneys' and extending smokeboxes, tenders and cabs.

Particularly associated with Melton Constable was William Marriott. He had been involved with the railways in the area during the early 1880s, transferring to the M&GN in 1893, first as Engineer and Locomotive Superintendent and being additionally appointed Traffic Manager in 1919. During World War 1 his youngest son, who had been taken on as a pupil at Melton Constable, was killed in action, together with 115 other M&GN staff. Melton Constable undertook war work, working round the clock with depleted staff to produce munitions while assisting Derby and Doncaster with repairs and building new wagons for the war effort overseas. During the war William Marriott developed concrete for use as signal posts, station signs, fencing, sleepers and much more, before retiring in 1924.

Left: With LNER numbering and in black (goods) livery, ex-M&GN Class J93 0-6-0T No 016 is seen on shunting duties at Melton Constable in 1946. One of a batch of nine, the locomotive had been built at Melton Constable in 1905 and was destined to be the last survivor of its class, being taken out of service in 1949 without receiving its allocated BR number. Note the connecting rod to the second pair of wheels. *P. Ward*

Above: A general view of Melton Constable, with evidence of shunting in the distance, on 16 April 1947. Note that the platform has been lengthened. The population of Melton Constable in 1881 was 118 but with the coming of the railway rose to a peak of over 1,200, most of whom were employed on the railway. By 1955 this figure had reduced to 866 and by 2001 was down to 518. *H. C. Casserley*

Centre right: Melton Constable was the key junction on the line for passenger trains to make connections, and this resulted in some lulls between periods of intense activity. The 'Leicesters' were the main expresses on the line to and from the Midlands, but long-distance trains to and from London Liverpool Street and King's Cross also provided connections at Melton Constable. Here ex-GER Class D15 4-4-0 No 62520 has arrived with a busy train. The view is undated, but judging by the crowds and the wet weather it may just be a holiday period in the early 1950s. The water towers seen on the left survive today. *Ian Allan Library*

Right: Ivatt Class 4MT 2-6-0 No 43142 with a freight train at Melton Constable on 15 July 1952. Freight was of great importance to the line, coal being brought in from the Midlands and agricultural produce despatched in the opposite direction — flowers in spring, soft fruit, potatoes and vegetables in summer, grain, apples and plums in autumn and sugar beet in winter. The buildings behind the locomotive survive. *B. Lockey*

Table 52   MELTON CONSTABLE and NORWICH (City)

Miles		Week Days only					Miles		Week Days only			
		am am	am am	pm (V S)	pm pm pm pm (B)				am am	am am (B)	pm pm pm pm (J L)	pm (F)
—	Melton Constable .. dep	6 36 7 49	9 37 1041	1224 1 32	4 3 5 6 23 7 25		—	Norwich (City) .. dep	6 28 7 41	9 31 1032	1 23 4 52 5 32 7 16	10 45
2	Hindolvestone	6 40 7 53	9 42 1045	1228 1 36	4 7 5 9 7 29		4½	Drayton	6 37 7 50	9 40 1041	1 32 5 15 43 7 25	1053
4½	Guestwick	6 46 7 59	9 48 1051	1234 1 42	4 13 5 15 7 35		9	Attlebridge	6 46 7 59	1050	1 41 5 105 52 7 34	11 3
8½	Whitwell and Reepham	6 56 8 10	9 58 11 2	1242 1 52	4 21 5 23 36 7 44		10½	Lenwade	6 50 8 3	9 51 1054	1 45 5 145 56 7 38	11 7
10½	Lenwade	7 1 8 15	10 3 11 8	1247 1 57	4 26 5 28 41 7 49		13	Whitwell and Reepham	6 55 8 9	9 57 11 0	1 51 5 24 6 2 7 48	1122
12½	Attlebridge	7 6 8 20	10 8 1112	1252 2 2	4 31 5 33 7 54		16½	Guestwick	7 9 8 18	10 6 11 9	2 0 5 33 6 11 7 57	1127
16¾	Drayton	7 15 8 29	1017 1121	1 2 2 11	4 40 5 42 52 8 3		19¼	Hindolvestone	7 15 8 23	11 14	2 5 5 38 6 16 8 2	1127
21¼	Norwich (City) .... arr	7 23 8 37	1025 1129	1 9 2 19	4 48 5 50 7 08 14		21¼	Melton Constable .. arr	7 21 8 30	1014 1119	2 10 5 43 6 21 8 7	11 32

B Through Carriages from or to Birmingham (New Street) (Table 50)
F To Weybourne arr 11 53 pm (Table 51)
J To Fakenham (West) arr 6 45 pm (Table 50)
K From Holt dep 7 35 am (Table 51)
L To King's Lynn arr 9 30 pm (Table 50)
S Calls to set down only
V From Weybourne dep 12 0 pm (Table 51)

Following the Grouping in 1923 engineering work at Melton Constable continued, while shunting operations were regularly working to capacity. Few changes ensued initially under the new LMS/LNER regime, but in 1936 the committee agreed that the LNER should assume overall control. Thereafter LNER locomotives increasingly replaced those native to the M&GN, and in December 1936 the works closed other than to effect minor repairs to locomotives, carriages and wagons. Most workers were found other jobs, but there was dismay at the decision, for until then the works had provided the principal employment in the village and surrounding rural area.

World War 2 resulted in further changes, and by 1951 the last ex-M&GN locomotives had been withdrawn. Under BR there nevertheless remained a locomotive shed (32G) at Melton Constable, which in 1950 could still boast an allocation of 26. However the postwar years witnessed a decline in both passenger and freight traffic.

In 1956 DMUs were introduced on the Norwich–Melton Constable route, boosting passenger numbers by 10%, but the railway was still losing money, and eventually the decision was taken to close it. Objections failed to save it, and 28 February 1959 saw the closure of the locomotive shed at Melton Constable, coinciding with the withdrawal of passenger services on all ex-M&GN lines save that to Cromer. The surviving Melton Constable–Sheringham section finally lost its passenger service on 6 April 1964, freight traffic ceasing in December. The distinctive former railway cottages remain, as do many of the one-time works buildings, but in terms of the rail network Melton Constable has reverted to being a remote Norfolk village.

Above: Melton Constable–Norwich City timetable, April 1955.

Left: The Cromer Beach portion of the 1.45pm from Birmingham, leaving Melton Constable on 18 July 1958 behind Class B12/3 4-6-0 No 61514. Melton Constable was one of just a handful of ex-M&GN stations to survive the February 1959 passenger closure, only to lose its remaining service in 1964. *Ian Allan Library*

Left: Heading in the direction of Norwich on 8 August 1958, Ivatt Class 4MT 2-6-0 No 43110 runs through Melton Constable with a freight, passing a Metro-Cammell DMU for Sheringham at the platform. By this time Ivatt Moguls had taken over most duties, and closure of the majority of the route in 1959 released many of these relatively modern locomotives for use elsewhere on the BR network. *F. Church*

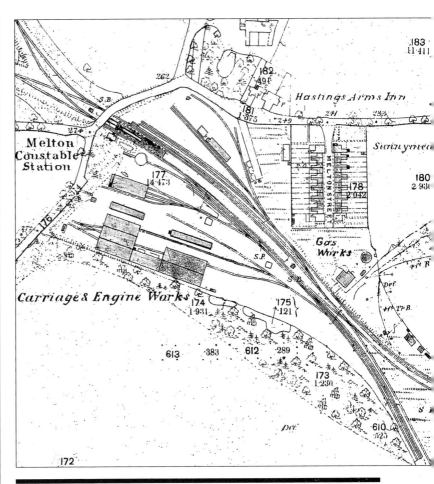

Above: Melton Constable prior to 1900. Further development was to follow.
Crown copyright

Left: Departures from Melton Constable in April 1956.

Below: The signs from both Melton signalboxes, as preserved in the William Marriott Railway Museum at Holt, on the North Norfolk Railway. Melton Constable was often referred to as just 'Melton'. *courtesy M&GN Society collection*

MELTON
CONSTABLE (Norfolk)

Miles 130¾. Map Sq. 14.
Pop. 866. Clos. day Thur.
REFRESHMENT ROOMS.
From Liverpool Street via King's Lynn.
1st cl.—Single 30/5, Return 60/10.
3rd cl.—Single 20/3, Return 40/6.

Liv. St.	M. Con.	M. Con.	Liv. St.
a.m.		a.m.	
8 24r	1 23	8 35r	1 33
9 54s	3 28	11 48	4 52
p.m.		p.m.	
2 24r	7 3	8 12	2 23
5 54r	10 48	—	—
7 24sr	12 0	—	—

No Sunday Trains.

r Refreshment Car.
s Saturday only.

Another Route.

From King's Cross via Peterborough.
1st cl.—Single 34/2, Return 68/4.
3rd cl.—Single 22/9, Return 45/6.

Kg's X	M.Con.	M.Con.	Kg's X
a.m.		a.m.	
3 50	9 24	8 35er	1 3
8 20r	1 23	8 35sr	1 10
10 20r	3 28	10 28q	4 12
p.m.		11 48mr	3 50
2 0r	6 15	11 48qr	4 48
6 18r	10 48	p.m.	
—	—	2 22f	7 25
—	—	2 22r	7 34

No Sunday Trains.

e Not Saturday *f* Friday only.
m Monday, Friday & Saturday.
q Tuesday, Wednesday & Thurs.
r Refresh. Car. *s* Saturday only.

Another Route.

From Liverpool Street via Norwich.
1st cl.—Single 36/3, Return 72/6.
3rd cl.—Single 24/2, Return 48/4.

Liv. St.	M. Con.	M. Con.	Liv. St.
a.m.		a.m.	
4 35	11 10	7 12r	11 23
9 30r	2 12	9 39k¶r	2 4
10 30r	3 40	9 39s¶r	2 6
p.m.		9 39f¶r	2 13
12 30sr	4 58	11 52er	4 34
12 30er	5 16	11 52sr	4 46
1 30r	7 6	p.m.	
3 30r	7 54	2 30r	7 45
5 30r	9 39	4 38	9 9
6 30m¶r	11 15	8 10	2 23
—	—	—	—
—	—	—	—

No Sunday Trains.

¶ "The East Anglian" between
   London and Norwich; limited
   bookings.
e Not Saturday.
f Friday only.
k Not Friday or Saturday.
m Monday, Friday & Saturday.
r Refreshment Car.
s Saturday only.

13 Journey's end

It is perhaps fitting that the 13th chapter of the 13th volume of the 'Lost Lines' series should feature the author's grandfather, Harry Welbourn. He was born on 13 August 1886 and farmed at Fleet Fen, on the M&GN. At the age of 39 and after 13 years of marriage he died of pneumonia — on 13 May 1926. Thirteen was unlucky for him. It was perhaps equally unlucky that some lines should have closed when they did, for had they survived only a little longer they might have been spared.

The closure of a railway is in many respects akin to death: suddenly the platforms are deserted and desolate, trains that brought friends together will never pass by again, the lamps are ousted, the clocks are stopped, and a silent, sad spirit pervades the decaying fabric. In valedictory mode we forgive shortcomings and fondly remember the good times, but sadly things can never be quite the same again.

An inscription on the day of near-total closure of the M&GN read: 'The M&GN will never die, only fade away'. Today much of the M&GN has ceased to exist, and parts have faded away into the landscape. Yet it is said that you are not really dead until you are forgotten. The M&GN is certainly not forgotten, nor has interest in the railway faded away, witness the many books and articles, village signs and an active preservation movement.

Another last-day inscription read: 'I will never pass this way again'. This may have seemed apposite at the time, but in the intervening half-century long sections of M&GN trackbed have been transformed into roads and footpaths, and between Holt and Sheringham even the clatter of steam trains has returned. Clearly, for the M&GN there is life after death.

Right: The diminutive Hindolvestone signalbox, located next to the level crossing, was still well maintained when photographed on 23 April 2009. Although no passengers were ever killed on the M&GN, one of the line's few accidents, involving slight injuries, occurred near here in 1937 when a train was derailed. *Author*

Below: Great Yarmouth Beach was journey's end for many passengers. This dramatic photograph of a surviving platform-canopy support, with cast-iron M&GN insignia, was taken in August 1994, by which time the station site was being used as a bus park. Following closure of the passenger station some buildings were retained for a time, but today few traces remain. *Author*

Above right: The larger signalbox at Langor Bridge, photographed in the direction of Melton Constable on 23 April 2009. A public siding was provided for local goods here, and at one time the signalbox also controlled the level crossing over the A1067 road. The steps up to most signalboxes had metal toe-plates inscribed 'M&GN'. *Author*

Right: The level-crossing gate at Lenwade —one of four once controlled by the signalbox — on 23 April 2009; note the open red diamond, which replaced the more usual solid red disk on most M&GN level crossings. The line at Lenwade was one of the last to close to freight, in June 1983, and the trackbed now forms a long-distance footpath known as the Marriott Way. *Author*

Left: The view west at Sutton Bridge, showing the island platform and rusting track after closure. The structure seen here dated mainly from 1897. This was the first photograph of a lost line taken by the author, as a schoolboy and with a borrowed camera, more than half a century ago! *Author*

Above: Although Sutton Bridge station was razed to the ground following closure, relics can still be found. This photograph was taken in July 2009 at the Winchcombe Railway Museum in Gloucestershire and shows a mile and yard post, here set at zero, used to indicate the distance to and from the bridge. Other M&GN mileposts at Sutton Bridge indicated 26 miles, the distance from Wisbech Junction. *Author*

Left: 'Stop and Think', a useful cast-iron sign in the control cabin situated above the swing bridge at Sutton Bridge, in August 1994. In March 1959 demolition contractors moved in, just 36 hours after the last train, to remove track east of Sutton Bridge, thereby ending the line's status as a through route and thwarting any plans for preservation here. *Author's collection*

Right: The distinctive brick-built former station building at Holbeach. The wooden buildings on the up side were demolished following closure of the line in May 1965. For a time this building was used by a printing firm, and after it vacated the premises plans to convert the station building into flats staved off the threat of demolition. In November 2009 the station seen here, along with the adjoining Station Hotel, remained derelict. *Author*

Right: The derelict Gedney station, in an isolated position some way from the village it purported to serve. Dating from 1862, it was a crossing-point on a section of single line. One of the large station signs, produced at Melton Constable, was still in evidence when this photograph was taken in November 2009, more than 50 years after closure. *Author*

Right: The M&GN saw some interesting uses following its demise as a railway. This photograph, taken on 6 August 1984, shows the eastern portal of the 330yd (302m) Toft (or Bourne) Tunnel, which had been deliberately flooded for use as an agricultural reservoir and nature reserve. *Author's collection*

The M&GN and GER eventually came together to build two lines that neither could really have justified individually, by means of the formation of the Norfolk & Suffolk Joint Railway. As the railway was an offspring of the M&GN it was a joint railway belonging to a joint railway! It never had its own stock, but did have its own staff, seal and stationery.

There were two lines, the first, running wholly within Norfolk, from North Walsham to the coast at Mundesley, opening in July 1898. In July 1906 this was extended to Cromer, by means of a single line with crossing-points at Trimingham and Overstrand.

Opened in July 1903, the second, entirely separate line, providing an 11-mile double-track link between Lowestoft and Yarmouth, crossed the Norfolk/Suffolk boundary and thereby provided the name for the whole joint enterprise. In order to connect Lowestoft with Yarmouth Beach the line at Breydon Water crossed a tidal inlet of the River Yare. North of Gorleston Junction the line was 'pure' M&GN, and the 800ft viaduct was the most important engineering work on the entire M&GN system, consisting of four fixed spans and a double-track swing span on a central pier.

Both lines developed summer-holiday passenger traffic, and in 1914 a further halt was provided at Gorleston Links. On the debit side, Gorleston North station was so badly damaged during World War 2 that it was closed permanently in October 1942. After the war a decline set in, and economies were effected, Breydon North and South signalboxes (protecting Breydon Viaduct) being replaced by single-line block working from Caister Road signalbox. In 1953 the viaduct was found to be in need of repair and was closed to all traffic with effect from 20 September. It was subsequently decided not to repair the structure,

and demolition was finally undertaken during 1962/3.

Economies were also made on the Mundesley line, tickets being issued on the train at Paston & Knapton, Trimingham and Overstrand, but the Mundesley–Cromer section was the first to close, in April 1953. Between 1953 and 1956 steam-hauled/propelled push-pull units worked the remaining section, which was now worked on the 'one engine in steam' principle. In 1956 the steam service was replaced by DMUs with conductor guards, allowing the ticket office at Mundesley to close.

In 1959, when the ex-GER line from Beccles to Yarmouth via St Olaves closed, trains were diverted onto the ex-N&S Lowestoft–Yarmouth South Town route, providing this line with its best-ever service. However, all the former joint lines were identified by Dr Beeching for closure, and the remaining link to Mundesley closed in December 1964. The Lowestoft–Yarmouth line initially survived, although it was singled and the stations became unstaffed.

Subsequent closure proposals for the Yarmouth–Lowestoft line met with anger, and a fight was mounted. However, although the East Suffolk line south to Ipswich was reprieved there was no saving the ex-N&S route, and the last train from Yarmouth South Town to Lowestoft ran in May 1970. Your author was on board and filmed with a movie camera the large crowds that came out to greet the train at every station.

Today little remains, all the N&S stations having been demolished with the exception of those at Overstrand and Paston & Knapton, which survive as private residences. At Cromer the short section of line linking Roughton Road Junction and Newstead Lane Junction is still used by trains between Norwich and Sheringham.

Left: Mundesley station was designed by William Marriott of the M&GN and with its graceful clock tower was generally recognised as one of the most elegant in East Anglia. Construction of this spacious facility, with three through platforms and a bay on the up side, anticipated significant growth in coastal holiday traffic; in 1933 six camping coaches were positioned here, but in 1953 the coastal route to Cromer closed, reducing Mundesley to a terminus. This photograph was taken at some time between 1956, when DMUs were introduced, and closure in 1964. *D. Lawrence*

MUNDESLEY-ON-SEA (Norfolk)

Miles 136¼. Map Sq. 14.
Pop. 990. Clos. day Wed.
From Liverpool Street via North Walsham.
1st cl.—Single 32/-, Return 64/-.
3rd cl.—Single 21/4, Return 42/8.

Liv. St.	Mund.	Mund.	Liv. St.
a.m.			a.m.
4 35	10 22	6 41r	10 0
9 30er	12 40	7 52sr	11 23
9 30sr	12 56	8 28sr	12 53
10 30sr	2 30	8 28er	12 56
p.m.		10 27k¶r	2 4
12 30sr	3 57	10 27s¶r	2 6
12 30er	4 23	10 27f¶r	2 13
1 30r	6 7	p.m.	
3 30r	6 41	12 24sr	4 46
5 30r	8 52	12 43er	4 34
—	—	1 40r	4 55
—	—	3 5sr	7 45
—	—	4 35sr	8 5
—	—	5 30	9 9
—	—	8 15	2 23

No Sunday Trains.

¶ "The East Anglian" between London and Norwich ; limited bookings.
e Not Saturday.   f Friday only.
k Not Friday or Saturday.
r Refreshment Car.
s Saturday only.
Buses from Norwich, Surrey Street Bus station, approx. every two hours (1 journey Sunday morning), 85 min. journey.

Grand Hotel. Leading. Finest Position, with Sea and Country Views. Nearest Links. Hard Tennis Courts. Billiards. Garage. A.A. and R.A.C.

Manor Hotel. 'Phone : 9. All Modern Amenities.

Above: Departures from Mundesley-on-Sea, April 1956.

Top: Trimingham station in April 1953, with the 1.10pm train from Sheringham to Norwich via Mundesley, hauled by Class D16/3 4-4-0 No 62617. The crossing loop dictated the provision of an island platform, which between summer and winter months saw a significant variation in patronage. The cutting seen here has been filled in since closure of the railway. *Ian Allan Library*

Above: Overstrand station in 1914, showing the subway access to the island platform. It was from Overstrand that Winston Churchill contacted the Admiralty to mobilise the fleet when World War 1 broke out, before rushing back to London by special train — a journey that is reputed locally to have taken just 1hr 55min. *Ian Allan Library*

Left: A derelict Overstrand station on 20 June 1959, some six years after closure. At one time a new resort was planned just south of Overstrand, and indeed a halt was opened at Sidestrand in 1936, but these plans were frustrated by the refusal of a key property-owner to sell his land. Following World War 2 (during which the station was again used by Winston Churchill, who stayed at the nearby Sea Marge Hotel) stretches of the coast here were not cleared of mines for some time, and this damaged holiday traffic on the railway. *A. Jackson*

Above left: Sadly, Mundesley station was demolished after closure, the cleared site being seen here on 4 August 1976. In 2010 this location remains largely unchanged and undeveloped, perhaps giving credence to those who had warned that this was a very quiet part of the country in which to build a railway. *Author*

Above: The site of Trimingham station, recorded on 4 August 1976. The overbridge, constructed of blue engineering brick, survives in 2010, although the station site has been built upon, and the cutting to the south filled in. *Author*

Left: Overstrand station was a crossing-point on the single line and remains largely as it was when closed, complete with glass-roofed subway and island platform buildings. Together with Paston & Knapton it is one of just two surviving ex-N&S stations. This photograph, taken on 4 July 2008, features one of the decorative N&S spandrels. *Author*

Right: The Lowestoft–Yarmouth section of the N&S passed through Gorleston-on-Sea. In early BR livery and with temporary number, ex-MSLR Class F2 2-4-2 No E7109 (later 67109) is seen pausing at the station on 17 May 1948 with the 2.50pm Lowestoft–Yarmouth Beach service. The train would travel over Breydon Viaduct to reach Yarmouth Beach station. *W. A. Camwell*

Above: Corton station in April 1970. By this time the ex-N&S line between Lowestoft and Yarmouth had been singled, and a basic 'pay train' service introduced whereby conductor-guards issued tickets on the train, all intermediate stations being reduced to unstaffed halts. However, such measures provided insufficient to save it, and despite considerable protest the railway closed in May 1970. *Author*

Left: Gorleston-on-Sea station was well placed for the town and only ⅛ mile from the sea. Although used as a private residence following closure in 1970, it was later demolished to make way for a road. This photograph, taken in August 1994, shows it in poor condition prior to demolition. *Author*

15 Great Northern & Great Eastern Joint Committee

This railway line was constructed as a result of the GER's desire for a freight route to the north for its agricultural products from East Anglia (and return traffic in coal), while the GNR for its part was keen to limit the GER's expansion aspirations and considered a joint operation a better option than a 'pure' GER line.

Thus was born the third-largest joint system, which eventually extended to 123 miles. It was not a separate corporate body but was run by a joint committee, comprising five representatives from each company, established in July 1879 after a possible merger between the GNR and GER was abandoned. The line formally became a joint concern in 1882 but was essentially a route over which both the GN and GE ran their own trains.

Starting at Huntingdon and proceeding east to St Ives, the joint line ran north from Needingworth Junction to March and thence to Spalding. From here it was extended to Lincoln (this section being open by August 1882) and eventually to Black Carr Junction, at Doncaster. Parts of it were purely GER- or GNR-owned, and despite the fact that the route ran parallel with the East Coast main line freight was particularly heavy on the March–Doncaster section. There was also a single-track branch from Somersham to Ramsey, opened in September 1889.

At the Grouping the line lost its joint status, becoming wholly owned by the LNER.

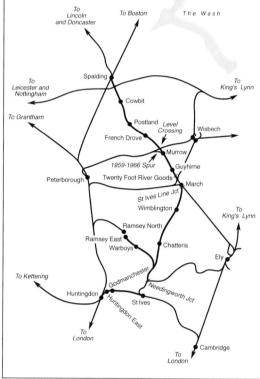

Left: The GN&GE joint line started out from Huntingdon in the south and was originally double track. However, weight restrictions on bridges over the River Ouse necessitated the use of light locomotives, and only local services used the Huntingdon–St Ives section. Seen shortly after leaving Huntington East with a short goods train to St Ives on 14 June 1958 is a relatively new BR 0-6-0 diesel shunter, No D2005. *F. Church*

The route reinforced the importance of March as a rail centre, and in 1929 the already extensive sidings at Whitemoor, just to the north, were replaced by a gravity-worked yard with the first rail retarders in Britain, the down yard being similarly equipped in 1933. By 1953 the capacity of the Whitemoor yards was some 7,000 wagons a day.

The Somersham–Ramsey East branch was an early casualty, being closed to passengers in September 1930 and to freight in August 1957, although part of the line, to Warboys, remained open until July 1964. The line from St Ives to Godmanchester was next to close, in June 1959, mainly because of weak wooden river bridges (some necessitating a 10mph speed restriction, even with light engines), and the surviving stub from Godmanchester to Huntington followed in June 1962. The Needingworth Junction–March section, was abandoned in March 1967. Perhaps surprisingly the next closure — that of the direct line between March and Spalding — was not until 27 November 1982, following which all trains had to travel via Peterborough. The following year saw the closure of the Lincoln-avoiding line, but that at Sleaford survived, albeit as a single track and unused in 2009.

Despite the closures of some sections, much of the former joint line has survived remarkably well, and the Spalding–Doncaster section remains open, on account of previous and potential freight use. Passenger services were always limited and were not run over the entire length of the 'Joint Line', as it is still sometimes known, the Huntingdon–St Ives and St Ives–March services being separate from those north of March. Although local passenger services on the northern section were limited, and numerous small intermediate stations were closed, the route was used for many years by long-distance trains between East Anglia (notably Harwich) and the North.

When your author travelled over this line in April 1965 he noted particularly the old gas lamps at Spalding but also how few lights were to be seen from the train at night — a reminder that the line runs through a remote rural area. Repeating the journey in April 2008, he was struck by the lack of investment in the line: Spalding's station urinals were of the old huge porcelain variety, concrete-post semaphore signals were still in existence (albeit about to be replaced in the Lincoln area), and gated crossings and disused telegraph poles abounded.

Above right: Somersham station in September 1964, photographed (in the direction of St Ives) from a Cambridge–March DMU service. This service used the Needingworth Junction–March section of the ex-GN&GE joint line. Somersham had been the junction for the Ramsey East branch, on which surviving freight traffic ceased in July 1964. *Author*

Right: Joint lines cross at Murrow. Bound for the ex-M&GN yard with a brake van, Ivatt Class 4MT 2-6-0 No 43105 passes Murrow West signalbox as it crosses the ex-GN&GE joint line on 21 May 1957. In February 1927 this was the scene of a collision between two goods trains, fortunately without fatalities. Upon closure of the majority of ex-M&GN network in 1959 a new spur was built, enabling freight to continue from Murrow to Wisbech Harbour and a brick works until April 1966. *Ian Allan Library*

G.E.R. **SP**

From _____ TO _____

via G.N. & G.E. Joint Line
and Spalding.

2nd-SINGLE

1966

March Chatteris

March

CHATT

(E) 2/6 Far

For conditions see over

L. N. E. R.
EXCHANGE TICKET
FOR CONDITIONS SEE BACK
ST. IVES (HUNTS) to
HUNTINGDON EAST
Available only on date shewn hereon.
Available at intermediate station. Issued in
exchange for return half of Eastern National
Bus Co's, Ltd., Ticket No..............

THIRD CLASS SUPPLEMENT 2½d.

Above: Class B16/2 4-6-0 No 61475 heads into Spalding with a freight train from March over the ex-GN&GE joint line on 29 April 1958. The ex-M&GN avoiding line, opened in 1893, can be seen in the background. The footbridge from which this photograph was taken survives and is featured later in this chapter. *P. Wells*

Left: The same view on 21 August 1964. Brush Type 2 No D5629 heads towards Spalding from March with a train of four-wheeled vans. Freight was particularly important on this route, especially agricultural produce going north and coal from Yorkshire going south. Note the demolition of the bridge on the ex-M&GN avoiding line in the background, after closure in 1959. The general area seen here is now partly developed with housing. *P. Wells*

Above: Class 37 No 37 075 passes French Drove, between March and Spalding, with the 14.31 Summer Saturdays Yarmouth–Sheffield on 3 July 1982. By this time the two loops at this location were little used, the route having gradually lost status and traffic. Lack of investment ensured that concrete-post semaphore signals continued to be a feature of this line until closure. *B. Beer*

Above: The former joint line at Guyhirne, seen in January 1983. At the time closure between March and Spalding, effected two months previously, seemed like a saving, but the line is now acknowledged to have provided a useful link, and consideration has even been given to its reopening. Guyhirne station closed to passengers in October 1953 and was subsequently demolished. The bridge in the distance carried the line over the River Nene. *Ian Allan Library*

GN & GE
36

Right: The Class 40 'Whistlers' enjoyed a long association with the ex-GN&GE route. Here No 40 152 passes through French Drove station with the 09.40 Monk Bretton–Middleton Towers sand empties on 20 November 1982. Most small passenger stations on the line were of a distinctive brick design. French Drove had closed to passengers in September 1961, but the buildings survive as a private residence. *J. Rudd*

Left: Somersham station level crossing in August 1994, after demolition of all but the station house (although one of the main wooden platform buildings was later re-erected at a private museum in Oxfordshire). The tall concrete gate post remained in 2009, some 45 years after your author first visited the site. *Author*

Left: The only branch on the GN&GE Joint line ran from Somersham to Ramsey. This photograph shows Ramsey East station following final closure (in 1957) and removal of the track. The station itself has since been demolished, and the site redeveloped. *D. Lawrence*

Left: Postland station signalbox, photographed on 15 August 2008. The 'box retains its levers, and there were once plans for it to be dismantled and shipped to America. However, these have apparently long since been abandoned, and the structure is now in a dilapidated condition. Postland station closed to passengers in September 1961, but although the track has gone, having been lifted following closure of the March–Spalding line in 1983, the station buildings were still largely intact at the time of the author's visit. *Author*

Above: At Murrow some station buildings remain on the joint lines, as does this modern-design signalbox, photographed on 15 August 2008. Murrow has as its village sign crossed rails and an M&GN locomotive. *Author*

Right: Footbridge over the M&GN and GN&GE alignments south of Spalding station, photographed on 16 July 2008. The iron arches above the walkway may originally have supported gas lamps. *Author*

16 Ashby & Nuneaton Joint Railway

The quiet undulating countryside near Market Bosworth belies a bloody past, most notably the death in battle of Richard III at nearby Bosworth Field. However, there were later battles in the area. The Ashby Canal opened in 1804, and a network of tramways once conveyed coal from the Leicestershire coalfield to the canal. With the coming of the railways there was a battle with the canal to win its customers. Those two great railway rivals, the LNWR and the MR, also had their battles but came together in this area to provide the only significant joint line in which they collaborated.

The Ashby & Nuneaton Joint Railway was formed because both the LNWR and MR had proposed similar lines in this coalfield area. The LNWR and MR both had their own lines in the Coalville and Nuneaton areas, and they eventually opened the 29¼-mile joint lines to all traffic in September 1873. Although the railway did not directly serve Ashby, it did improve communications around the Ashby Wolds area. It also served increasing numbers of collieries, gradually reducing the use of the canal.

The principal joint route left the MR Burton–Leicester line at Moira West Junction and ran south to Nuneaton, where, at Ashby Junction, it joined the LNWR main line, the short Weddington Junction spur allowng access to the MR station. There was also a line linking Stoke Golding and Hinckley, but this was never used. The other significant section of the joint railway was a single-line branch that meandered from Shackerstone Junction to Hugglescote, from where links were provided to Loughborough and the Midland main line at Coalville. Also owned by the joint railway was an altogether separate 2¾-mile freight-only branch line, opened in 1893, from Narborough, on the Nuneaton–Leicester line, to a quarry at Enderby.

The main joint line provided a number of convenient links, and Shackerstone Junction developed as the headquarters of the joint railway. While the railway was worked with the locomotives and stock of both partners, stations and staff uniforms on the joint line were designed to a distinctive pattern, which reflected both the LNW and Midland railways. In 1880 Queen Victoria travelled over the line, while King Edward VII used it to visit nearby Gopshall Hall (since demolished).

Prior to the Grouping regular passenger services between Nuneaton and Ashby and Burton-upon-Trent were operated by both the LNW and Midland railways. The Shackerstone–Coalville line was worked by LNWR motor trains, but these ceased in April 1931, some years after the LMS had taken over as sole owner of the joint line. This date also saw the end of regular passenger trains on the Moira–Nuneaton section, but excursions were run until the early 1960s.

Surviving goods services on the Shackerstone–Hugglescote section, which in the heyday of the joint line had included heavy coal traffic, were withdrawn in April 1964, while the Moira–Nuneaton section saw a dwindling number of freight trains and closed altogether as a through route in August 1969. Parts of the latter were used as a wagon store until July 1971, when the line south of Market Bosworth closed completely, while the Market Bosworth–Measham section was taken out of use in November of that year. The final Measham Colliery–Moira West Junction section was singled in 1972 and closed in June 1981, outlasting the isolated branch to Enderby, which succumbed in April 1980.

Today the Shackerstone–Shenton section has been preserved as the Battlefield Line Railway. The Ashby Canal is also being restored, and, the rivalry with the railway being long forgotten, the two modes of transport will soon join together to provide a great day out.

Right: Ex-MR 0-6-0 Class 3F No 43251 passes through an increasingly derelict Shackerstone Junction with a lengthy coal train from the Moira line in the late 1950s. Moira coal was promoted for its quality and economy in use, producing little smoke, smell or cinders, and was used by many in the Midlands and South. Until 1944 it was also transported by the Ashby Canal, which owned its own fleet of barges that were at one time hauled by steam tugs. *Ian Allan Library*

Below right: Headed by Stanier Class 8F 2-8-0 No 48343, a southbound coal train leaves the single-track Coalville line at Shackerstone Junction in the late 1950s. The 36-lever MR-type signalbox here was demolished after closure of the line, while the trackbed on the far left of this view is now used as the main road access to the preserved Battlefield Line Railway. *Ian Allan Library*

Below: BR/Sulzer Type 2 No D7534 passes a derelict and overgrown Shackerstone station with a goods train from the Nuneaton direction on 11 September 1967. The distinctive design of the stations on this joint line incorporated a covered area within the station building. In the days when passenger services were provided, the MR and LNWR generally produced separate timetables for their respective services over the joint line. *M. Mitchell*

Left: Stanier Class 8F 2-8-0 No 48063 heads a southbound coal train on the single-line section between Snarestone and Shackerstone on 13 September 1965. Had the line not closed it could have provided a useful north–south trunk route for long-distance trains, avoiding the bottleneck of Birmingham. *M. Mitchell*

Below left: At Hugglescote the joint line linked up with the ex-LNWR branch to Loughborough. Here ex-LMS 'Crab' 2-6-0 No 42756 passes the derelict Hugglescote station, on the Coalville–Shackerstone line, with the SLS/MLS 'Leicestershire Rail Tour' of 8 September 1962. *G. King*

SHACKERSTONE RAILWAY SOCIETY LTD
THE BATTLEFIELD LINE

SHENTON   SHACKERSTONE
TO   TO
SHACKERSTONE   SHENTON

ADULT   **RETURN**

9718

Issued subject to the Company's regulations and notices NOT TRANSFERABLE

Above: Headed by ex-LMS Class 4F 0-6-0 No 44542, an excursion train from Burton-upon-Trent to Leamington Spa draws into Stoke Golding station in June 1953. The station had closed to regular passenger services in 1931 but would remain open until the early 1960s for goods and excursion traffic. *W. A. Camwell*

Left: Stoke Golding station detail, showing an oil-lamp bracket still *in situ* on 14 August 2008. The decorative protruding eaves and contrasting red, blue and yellow bricks show MR influence but were also distinctive features of some of the joint stations on the line. *Author*

Above: Measham station entrance on 14 August 2008. The elegant closed station had been restored from a derelict condition and was about to be put to community use when this photograph was taken. Measham pit had started to use the railway as late as 1902, when a siding was laid to the colliery. Almost all signs of the coal industry here have gone, but the line's joint stations and goods buildings have survived remarkably well. *Author*

17 Great Northern & London North Western Joint Railway

This 45-mile substantially built double-track joint line ran through a sparsely populated and rolling rural part of East Leicestershire. Although agricultural traffic developed, the area was rich in iron ore, and this was a key reason for the line's existence. Numerous iron-ore quarries, mines and works sidings could once be found leading off the main route, and the joint railway soon became heavily used by mineral trains.

The joint railway commenced at Welham Junction, on the LNWR line north-east of Market Harborough, and ran northwards to Melton Mowbray. It then tunnelled through the Harby Hills to Harby & Stathern station, where the line divided in the Vale of Belvoir,

the two forks joining the GNR Grantham–Nottingham line. At the southern end there was a spur from Hallaton, which also made direct contact with the LNWR line. The joint line was opened by the GN and LNW railways during 1879.

The railway allowed the LNWR access to Nottingham, by means of running powers over the GNR, and, conversely, gave the GNR access to Leicester and running powers over the LNWR to Northampton, these destinations all being outside the traditional territories of the respective railways. Over the main section of line the LNWR ran through trains to and from Northampton and Nottingham, and at one time there was also a through carriage to and from Melton Mowbray to Euston. The GNR link from the triangular set of junctions at Marefield to Leicester Belgrave Road was also used to run excursion trains over the joint line to Skegness and the Lincolnshire coast, while another GNR link from Bottesford provided direct access to Newark. Melton Mowbray North was the railway's headquarters, where the joint committee met, but Harby & Stathern, with a large yard and turntable, was the main station.

Passenger services in this remote area were never extensive. The short spur to Hallaton closed in 1916 as a wartime economy measure, but was destined never to reopen. The line remained in joint (LNER and LMS) ownership after the Grouping. Regular services to the mostly isolated rural stations on the line ceased in December 1953, but one, generally lightly loaded passenger train ran from Melton Mowbray to Leicester Belgrave Road and back until April 1957. Unadvertised workmen's trains also ran between Market Harborough and East Norton until May 1957, while summer excursions from Leicester Belgrave Road to Skegness and Mablethorpe continued until September 1962.

Freight declined as local iron-ore deposits became exhausted. The Saxondale Junction–Barnstone link closed in September 1962, while the remaining lines closed as a through route in September 1964, and the section south of Harby & Stathern was lifted. The Stathern ironstone siding closed in October 1967, to be followed in January 1968 by the Harby & Stathern, Barnstone and Redmile links. The Redmile–Bottesford section was used as a wagon store until December 1970.

The line was heavily constructed, and Clawson Tunnel and Marefield Viaduct survive, as do many of the substantial bridges on the route. However, almost all of the station buildings have been demolished, although the goods shed at the remote Harby & Stathern station remains, along with most former stationmaster's houses and other railway cottages at the intermediate stations.

On Sunday 25 April 1965 the author made a trip to Redmile station, noting in his diary that there were a large number of wagons at the station and that the nearby Grantham Canal, which had been abandoned in 1936, was heavily overgrown. A return visit in April 2008 revealed the canal to be less overgrown and that all the ex-railway housing at Redmile station had survived. However, a derelict brick hut deep in thick undergrowth was all that remained of the grand station, which once had an ornate private waiting room for the exclusive use of the occupants of nearby Belvoir Castle.

Above: Melton Mowbray North was once the headquarters of the GN&LNW Joint Railway. The station's First-class waiting room was panelled in oak, but the glory days were long gone by the time this Leicester Belgrave Road–Mablethorpe excursion train, hauled by ex-LNER Class B1 4-6-0 No 61092, was photographed arriving between the glassless iron canopies on 23 July 1955. The station was demolished in 1970, although a GNR crest from the station has been preserved at a Leicester museum. *R. Buckley*

Below: Melton Mowbray North station in 1902. The proximity of the cattle market (left) to the station is readily apparent. *Crown copyright*

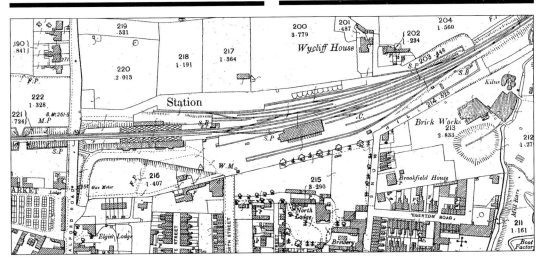

5

Above left: WD Austerity 2-8-0 No 90492 passes East Norton in August 1960 — after the station closed to regular passenger services — with the 8.15am Colwick–Sudbury Junction coal train. The substantial bridge parapets remain at East Norton, although as with many bridges on the line the void under the bridge arch has been filled in with earth and rubble. The buildings seen here have since been demolished, but the station's letterbox and the distinctive stationmaster's house (out of view to the right) all survive. *C. Walker*

Left: East Norton station on 2 May 1962, with WD Austerity 2-8-0 No 90717 hauling the 8am Welham Junction–Melton Mowbray freight. The station closed to regular passenger services in December 1953, but a Market Harborough–East Norton workmen's service ran until May 1957, and a number of summer excursion trains continued until September 1962. Agricultural freight was also important, and the old cattle dock can be seen on the left, just beyond the platform. The derelict passenger stations were a feature of this line. *P. Wells*

Above: View from the footplate of WD Austerity 2-8-0 No 90492, approaching Stathern Junction on 5 September 1961 with the 8.15am Colwick–Sudbury Junction goods. The line joining from the left is that from Bottesford via Redmile. The goods shed and other structures remain at the nearby Harby & Stathern station in 2010. *C. Walker*

Above right: A cast-iron GN&LNW Joint Committee notice alongside to the bridge between Scalford and Hose Tunnel. The cutting section seen here remains but is now heavily overgrown. *C. Walker*

Below: A 1950s view of Clawston Tunnel, 834yd (763m) long and sometimes known as Hose Tunnel, with an ex-GCR Class O4/8 2-8-0 approaching tender-first with a coal train. Steep gradients on this section of line could cause trains such as this to stall. After closure the tunnel was used partly as a farm store, although walking through it was still possible. Your author attempted to do so in 2009, but the northern approach was by then too heavily overgrown for this to be possible. *Hugh Davis*

Right: Lowesby station, although just off the GN&LNW, shared the general architectural design of the joint railway. Today it presents a striking contrast; the building on the up side has been restored to residential use, but that on the down side remains in a derelict condition, as apparent from this photograph, taken on 4 August 2008. A view of this building in better preserve can be found in *Lost Lines: Eastern.* *Author's collection*

Far right: The fine double-track, mainly red-brick viaduct between John O'Gaunt station and Marefield North Junction survives, this photograph dating from 4 August 2008. The 13 main arches, more than 60ft (18m) high, make an impressive sight in the landscape, but by the time of author's visit it was clear that parts of the structure were deteriorating. The John O'Gaunt station name was derived from a nearby fox covert, and at one time special trains, for spectators, huntsmen and horses, were run on the line. *Author*

Above: BR/Sulzer Type 2 No D5010 passes Welham Junction with a Birmingham–Lowestoft train on 30 March 1964, the tracks in the foreground (right) representing the southern extremity of the 45-mile former joint line. In common with the ex-LNWR line they would later be removed and the area returned to agricultural use. *M. Mitchell*

Right: Timetable for July 1955, revealing the sparseness of the passenger service.

Below: The mileage posts on the joint railway were particularly distinctive, being different from those of both parent companies. This example of the unique cast-iron shield design, which was set at an angle so as to be easily readable from locomotives, was photographed at Winchcombe Railway Museum in July 2009. *Author*

SEASIDE EXCURSION

TO

SUTTON-on-SEA

AND

MABLETHORPE

SUNDAY, 21st SEPTEMBER, 1952

FROM	TIMES OF DEPARTURE	RETURN FARES (Third Class) to Sutton-on-Sea or Mablethorpe
	a.m.	s. d.
LEICESTER (Belgrave Road) ...	9 45	10 0
HUMBERSTONE	9 51	10 0
THURNBY & S.	9 57	10 0
INGARSBY	10 5	10 0
LOWESBY	10 13	10 0
JOHN O'GAUNT	10 21	10 0
MELTON MOWBRAY (North) ...	10 37	8 3
	p.m.	
SUTTON-ON-SEA ... arrive	12 46	...
MABLETHORPE ... „	12 54	...

RETURN ARRANGEMENTS

Passengers return same day as under:—

Mablethorpe ... ... dep. 7.2 p.m.
Sutton-on-Sea ... ... „ 7.10 p.m.
(due Leicester (Belgrave Road) at 10.17 p.m.).

CHILDREN under three years of age, free; three years and under fourteen, half-fares.

CONDITIONS OF ISSUE

Day, Half-day and Evening tickets are issued subject to the conditions applicable to tickets of these descriptions as shown in the Bye-Laws and Regulations, General Notices, Regulations and Conditions exhibited at Stations, or where not so exhibited, copies can be obtained free of charge at the Station booking office.
For LUGGAGE ALLOWANCES also see these Regulations and Conditions.

TICKETS CAN BE OBTAINED IN ADVANCE AT STATIONS AND AGENCIES

Further information will be supplied on application to Stations, Agencies, or to Mr. H. TANDY, District Commercial Superintendent, Leicester. Telephone 5542, Extn. 34.

August, 1952
B.R. 35000

(PX2/Halfex)

Table 61 LEICESTER, MELTON MOWBRAY, SKEGNESS and MABLETHORPE

Miles		Week Days															Sundays		
		am Saturdays only. TC to Skegness			am Saturdays only TC to Sutton-on-Sea and Mablethorpe			pm Saturdays only			pm Except Saturdays						am Runs 26th June to 4th September inclusive TC to Skegness		
	Leicester (Belgrave Rd) dep	**8 25**	..	..	**8 45**	..	..	**1 0**	..	..	**6 10**	..	..	..	..	..	**9 25**	..	..
1¼	Humberstone	8 32	..	..	8 52	..	..	5	..	..	6 15	..	..	..	..	..	9 31	..	..
3½	Thurnby and Scraptoft	8 39	..	..	8 59	..	..	10	..	..	6 20	..	..	..	..	..	9 37	..	..
6¼	Ingarsby	..	..	..	..	..	..	16	..	..	6 26	..	..	..	..	..	..	..	..
9¼	Lowesby	..	..	..	..	..	..	22	..	..	6 32	..	..	..	..	..	..	..	..
11¼	John o'Gaunt	..	..	..	..	..	..	27	..	..	6 36	..	..	..	..	..	..	..	..
18¼	**Melton Mowbray** arr	**9 6**	..	..	**9 25**	..	..	..	..	..	..	..	..	..	..	..	**10 4**	..	..
	dep	**9 10**	..	..	**9 27**	..	..	..	..	..	..	..	..	..	..	..	**10 8**	..	..
33	Bottesford	..	..	..	9 55	..	..	..	..	..	..	..	..	..	..	..	..	..	..
72¼	**Boston** arr	**1035**	..	..	**1055**	..	..	..	..	..	..	..	..	..	..	..	..	..	..
96¾	**Skegness** "	**1118**	..	..	**1147**	..	..	..	..	..	..	..	..	..	..	..	**1214**	..	..
100	**Sutton-on-Sea** "	..	..	..	**1151**	..	..	..	..	..	..	..	..	..	..	..	..	..	..
102¾	**Mablethorpe** "	..	..	..	**12 2**	..	..	..	..	..	..	..	..	..	..	..	..	..	..
119¾	54 Grimsby Town arr	..	..	..	2 5	..	..	..	..	..	..	..	..	..	..	..	..	..	..

Miles from Mablethorpe	Miles from Skegness		Week Days															Sundays		
			am			pm Saturdays only. TC from Skegness				pm Saturdays only TC from Mablethorpe and Sutton-on-Sea								pm Runs 26th June to 4th September inclusive TC from Skegness		
		54 Grimsby Town dep	..	..	..	1233	..	..	..	..	..	..	..	..	..	..	..	..	..	..
		Mablethorpe dep	..	..	..	..	..	..	..	**1 50**	..	..	..	..	..	..	..	..	..	..
2¾		**Sutton-on-Sea** "	..	..	..	..	..	..	..	**1 58**	..	..	..	..	..	..	..	..	..	..
—		**Skegness** "	..	..	..	**1 42**	..	..	..	..	..	..	..	..	..	..	..	**7 16**	..	..
30½	24¼	**Boston** "	..	..	..	**2 24**	..	..	..	**2 46**	..	..	..	..	..	..	..	..	..	..
69¾	63½	Bottesford	..	..	..	..	..	..	..	3c50	..	..	..	..	..	..	..	..	..	..
84½	78¼	**Melton Mowbray** arr	..	..	..	**3 50**	..	..	..	**4 17**	..	..	..	..	..	..	..	**9 22**	..	..
		dep	..	..	..	**3 54**	..	..	..	**4 21**	..	..	..	..	..	..	..	**9 26**	..	..
91½	85¼	John o'Gaunt	7 50	..	..	..	..	..	..	..	..	..	..	..	..	..	..	..	..	..
93½	87¼	Lowesby	7 55	..	..	..	..	..	..	..	..	..	..	..	..	..	..	..	..	..
96½	90¼	Ingarsby	8 1	..	..	..	..	..	..	..	..	..	..	..	..	..	..	..	..	..
99¼	93	Thurnby and Scraptoft	8 7	..	..	4c21	..	..	..	4c48	..	..	..	..	..	..	..	9 54	..	..
101½	95¼	Humberstone	8 12	..	..	4d30	..	..	..	4d57	..	..	..	..	..	..	..	10 1	..	..
102¾	96½	**Leicester** (Belgrave Rd) arr	**8 17**	..	..	**4 35**	..	..	..	**5 2**	..	..	..	..	..	..	..	**10 6**	..	..

c Arr 3 minutes *earlier* d Arr 4 minutes *earlier* **TC** Through Carriages

18 The fall of Victoria

There were a number of jointly stations in major cities, and of those closed Nottingham Victoria, which was managed by the Nottingham Joint Station Committee, of the GC and GN railways, is particularly interesting.

The station, in the centre of Nottingham, was located in a cavernous cutting carved out of rock, between two GCR tunnels. A substantial building, its construction required the demolition of 1,300 houses and took almost six years. The station was designed in Dutch Renaissance style, capped with a finely detailed and engineered clock tower, and its lavish scale, with three spans — two of 63ft (19m) either side of a central one of 84ft (25m) — rising to more than 40ft (12m) above the platforms, was seen as befitting Nottingham's newly granted city status. The grand opening, in May 1900, coincided with Queen Victoria's birthday, and it was thus called 'Victoria' rather than 'Central'. The adjoining Victoria Hotel, in a matching but plainer style, was completed by 1901 but was not in direct railway ownership.

When the station was built rail traffic was still growing and it was designed to handle over 170 passenger trains a day, but its scale proved over-optimistic. It was never modernised to any great extent, and by the 1960s the decaying hulk, with its soot-stained glass and array of oil-lit lower-quadrant semaphore signals, presented a depressing sight.

In the end only a few local passenger and freight trains used the station's 12 platforms and freight avoiding lines. It was thus a prime candidate for Dr Beeching's rationalisation plan to close duplicated facilities. The ex-MR station at Nottingham was to become the key station, a new passenger link being provided to the ex-GNR line to Grantham. Although there were protests, Dr Beeching being portrayed as more wicked than the Sheriff of Nottingham, these were to no avail, and Nottingham Victoria duly closed in September 1967. The sole remaining DMU service to Rugby was transferred to nearby Arkwright Street but was itself withdrawn in 1969.

After closure the station building was soon demolished, and a 1960s-style shopping centre built on the site. Provision was made for two freight-only tracks through the development, but these were later removed, although the northern tunnel mouth and much of the blue-brick cutting walls can still be seen today. The hotel and station clock tower were also retained, looking rather elegant alongside the concrete structures of the 1960s.

Left: Nottingham Victoria station, in the heart of the city, was once a showpiece, spare capacity being used on this occasion for a railway exhibition of LNER locomotives. Exhibits included the new experimental 4-6-4, No 10000, and Gresley Class A1 Pacific No 4472 *Flying Scotsman*, seen here in immaculate condition on Sunday 10 May 1931. *Charles Macpherson*

NOTTINGHAM

Miles 123½. Map Sq. 13.
Pop. 306,008. Clos. day Thur.

Another Route
VICTORIA STATION.
REFRESHMENT ROOMS.
From Marylebone. Same fares.

M'bone	Nott.	Nott.	M'bone
a.m.		a.m.	
1 45	4‡58	1 40c	5 5
10 0r	12 52	8 39sr	11 25
p.m.		8 46er	11 23
12 15er	3 14	10 42er	1 41
12 15sr	3 21	10 42sr	1 55
3 20r	6 16	p.m.	
4 50r	7 36	12 34r	3 29
6 15sr	9 3	4 9r	7 10
6 18er	8 56	6 15r	9 20
10 0e	1 28	—	—
10 45s	1 41	—	—

Sunday Trains.

a.m.		a.m.	
12 45	4 13	1 40	5 5
8 10	12 37	9 55	1 30
9 50r	1 3	p.m.	
p.m.		12 40r	4 15
3 30r	6 59	4 55	8 43
8 5	11 25	6 0	9 12
10 55	2 34	6 15r	9 45

‡ Calls also at Arkwright Street
at 4.37 a.m.
c Not Monday. e Not Saturday.
r Refresh. Car. s Saturday only.
See overleaf.

NOTTINGHAM—*contd.*

Another Route
VICTORIA STATION.
From King's Cross via Grantham.
1st cl.—Single 30/2, Return 60/4.
3rd cl.—Single 20/1, Return 40/2.
Most Weekday trains call also at
Nottingham London Road station, 2
min. shorter journey. Same fares.

Kg's X	Nott.	Nott.	Kg's X
a.m.		a.m.	
3 50	7 26	6 22r	9 50
5 50	10 31	7 33	10 50
8 20r	11 46	8 25r	11 23
10 20sr	1 10	10 28r	1 30
10 20er	1 47	11 33br	3 2
p.m.		11 33r	3 17
12 18r	3 54	p.m.	
1 18r	5 0	1 45sr	4 48
3 20r	6 22	2 18r	5 35
3 52r	7 2	4 5r	7 34
5 35gr	8 50	6 10r	9 36
5 50fr	8 58	11 0	3 3
6 10r	9 39	—	—
6 50fr	10 51	—	—
7 0gr	10 51	—	—
8 20	12 2	—	—
—	—	—	—

Sunday Trains.

a.m.		a.m.	
7 45	11 43	11 0r	3 15
10 10r	2 2	p.m.	
p.m.		1 10r	4 30
3 0r	7 15	5 15r	8 40
6 0r	9 18	10 55	2 10
—	—	—	—
—	—	—	—
—	—	—	—

b Monday only. e Not Saturday.
f Friday only. g Not Friday.
r Refreshment Car.
s Saturday only.

Victoria Station Hotel. Largest
and Best. 'Phone: 43517 (5 lines). 'Grams
" Central."

Above: Nottingham Victoria was considered one of the finest provincial stations on the LNER. Here a gleaming ex-GCR Class D10 4-4-0 No 5430 *Purdon Viccars* is seen in charge of a down empty-stock working. The photograph was taken on 20 April 1939, and few could then have imagined that this fine main-line station would eventually be abandoned and demolished. *J. Henton*

Left: Departures from Nottingham Victoria to London Marylebone and London King's Cross, in April 1956.

Below: The lofty booking hall at Nottingham Victoria originally had seven ticket-issuing windows — three for each of the joint owning companies (GNR and GCR), and one for excursions. It is seen here in May 1953, being decorated for the coronation of Queen Elizabeth II. *Ian Allan Library*

Left: The first DMU service from Nottingham Victoria, the 10.26am to Grantham, departs on 19 September 1955; in the background is Class B1 4-6-0 No 61368. In July 1967 Grantham trains were re-routed to Nottingham Midland station, and in September of that year the last DMU left Victoria for Rugby. Ten days later the contractors moved in to demolish the station. *Ian Allan Library*

Left: Ex-LNER Class B1 4-6-0 No 61066 arrives at Nottingham Victoria on 29 August 1959 with a Saturdays-only Sheffield–Bournemouth West train, the carriages of which will travel over the S&D line to reach their destination. *J. Henton*

Left: A rather less cared-for WD 2-8-0, No 90103, heads through Nottingham Victoria with a northbound iron-ore train on 18 April 1964. Note the station clock tower in the background. *Ian Allan Library*

Right: Brush Type 4 No D1767 waits to leave Nottingham Victoria at 1.33am with the 9.55pm Marylebone–Manchester Piccadilly parcels on 19 February 1965. After closure of the station parcels were handled at the London Road Low Level terminus, which was cleaned and restored only for this traffic to be transferred to Platform 6 of the Midland station. In 2001 parcels traffic was withdrawn altogether. *N. Clarke*

Below right: The elegant clock tower built in Nottingham red pressed brick, with Darley stone dressing, was the only part of Victoria station saved from demolition, being restored to working order once the site had been redeveloped. This photograph was taken on 31 January 2008. *Author*

Below: The surviving ornamental door at the base of the clock tower, the latter of Dutch Renaissance style and giving a hint of the lavish architectural pretensions of the joint station. The tower has been incorporated into the aptly named Victoria Shopping Centre. *Author*

Bottom right: Base of an LNER Welch Patent oil-lit signal lamp, stamped with 'NOTTINGHAM V'. Almost all signalling at the station remained of a manual semaphore type until closure. Much of the equipment was inscribed, and at one time even the staff uniforms had 'NOTTINGHAM JOINT STATION' on the buttons. *Author's collection*

19 Axholme Joint Railway

The Goole & Marshland Light Railway, in north Lincolnshire, opened in stages from Marshland Junction, on the NER Thorne–Goole line, to Reedness, where it connected with the Isle of Axholme Light Railway from the GN&GE line at Haxey Junction.

Although this was a remote agricultural area it was also close to the River Humber, and both the LYR and NER recognised the potential strategic importance of these routes between the Humber ports and the Yorkshire collieries. As a consequence, although the original companies had obtained powers to construct lines under the terms of the Light Railway Act 1896, not all of these had been built by 1902, when they were purchased by the LYR and NER for operation as the Axholme Joint Railway — one of only two joint light railways in Britain. The LYR provided the motive power, while the NER assumed responsibility for the track.

The 'Marshland' and 'Island' titles of the original railway companies provide a clue that the Isle of Axholme was created by a series of rivers, and these all had to be crossed by the railway. Also required was a 104ft (34m) swing bridge over the Stainforth & Keadby Canal near Crowle.

The first line had been opened in January 1900, and by 1909 further construction had created a 27¾-mile network, comprising the Marshland Junction–Haxey Junction through line and two branches, from Reedness Junction to Fockerby and from Epworth to a peat works at Hatfield Moor, the latter being the last to

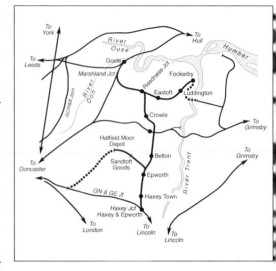

be completed. Proposed extensions to the North Lindsey Light Railway and from Hatfield Moor to Black Carr, to the east of Doncaster, came to nought.

By 1905 the main passenger service was that between Haxey Junction and Goole, with connections to Fockerby. Excursion trains were run to Epworth, the home of Methodism, but regular passengers were few, and in later years the Fockerby branch was reduced to just one train a day. After the Grouping the railway was owned jointly by the LMS and LNER. From 1926

Left: In 1930 a 100hp Sentinel-Cammell steam railcar was provided for passenger services. This could accommodate 64 passengers in reasonable comfort and had space for 10 more on tip-up seats in the luggage compartment. Finished in a livery of green and cream, with 'AXHOLME JOINT RAILWAY' emblazoned on the sides, it is seen here at Crowle in the early 1930s, the station buildings and level-crossing gates being behind the camera.
Ian Allan Library

the network was worked by a steam railcar, replaced by a larger car in 1930, but this could not halt the decline in passenger traffic in this remote rural area, and passenger services were withdrawn in July 1933.

The lines never became part of a through route for coal exports. Local agricultural produce and peat were the principal freight traffic, and this survived rather longer than the passenger services. The Epworth–Haxey Junction section was the first to close to freight, in February 1956, the Hatfield Moor branch following in September 1963, and the remaining sections, including Reedness Junction–Fockerby, closed in April 1965. Today some stretches of trackbed are used as footpaths, and several former station houses remain.

GOOLE, REEDNESS JUNCTION, FOCKERBY, CROWLE, and HAXEY JUNCTION (3rd class only).—Axholme Joint.
Secretary, H. Marriott, Hunt's Bank, Manchester. Supt., M. Woodhouse.

Mls	Down.	mrn	mrn (Sats. only.)	mrn (Wednesdays only.)	aft (Except Wednesdays.)	aft (Sats. only.)	aft (Except Saturdays.)	aft (Saturdays only.)
—	Goole ....dep.	7 8	9 25	1150	1218	3 5	5 30	5 45
5¼	Reedness Junction ....arr.	7 20	9 37	12 2	1230	3 17	5 42	5 57
—	Reedness Junction ..dep.	....		12 6	1234		5 46	6 1
8¾	Eastoft....	....		1215	1243		5 55	6 10
10	Luddington	....		1219	1247		5 59	6 14
11¼	Fockerby ....arr.	....		1223	1251		6 3	6 18
—	Reedness Junction ....dep.	7 21	9 38	12 4	1232	3 18	5 44	5 59
8½	Crowle 648, 654....	7 30	9 47	1213	1241	3 27	5 53	6 8
13	Belton....	7 42	9 59	1225	1253	3 39	6 5	6 20
14¾	Epworth	7 48	10 5	1231	1259	3 45	6 11	6 26
17¾	Haxey Town....	7 56	1013	1239	1 7	3 53	6 19	6 34
19½	Haxey Junction 389..arr.	8 0	1017	1243	1 11	3 57	6 23	6 38

Mls	Up.	mrn	mrn (Sats. only.)	aft (Wednesdays only.)	aft (Sats. only.)	aft (Except Wednesdays.)	aft (Sats. only.)	aft (Except Saturdays.)	aft (Saturdays only.)
—	Haxey Junction ....dep.	8 8	1043	1257		1 30	4 20	6 36	6 51
1¾	Haxey Town....	8 13	1048	1 2		1 35	4 25	6 41	6 56
4¾	Epworth	8 21	1056	1 10		1 43	4 33	6 49	7 4
6½	Belton....	8 28	11 3	1 17		1 50	4 40	6 56	7 11
10¾	Crowle....	8 40	1115	1 29		2 2	4 52	7 8	7 23
13¼	Reedness Junction ....arr.	8 48	1123	1 37		2 10	5 0	7 16	7 31
— Mls	Fockerby ....dep.	8 30		1 17	1 40	....		6 9	6 23
— 1¼	Luddington	8 34		1 21	1 44	....		6 13	6 27
— 2¾	Eastoft....	8 38		1 25	1 48	....		6 17	6 31
— 5½	Reedness Junction ..arr.	8 47		1 34	1 57	....		6 26	6 40
—	Reedness Junction ....dep.	8 53	112[illegible]	1 42	....	2 12	5 1	7 17	7 32
19½	Goole 721, 785....arr.	9 7	113[illegible]	1 55	....	2 24	5 15	7 29	7 45

Top: Axholme Joint Railway timetable, April 1910.

Above: The isolated location of Reedness Junction, amid the flat expanse of Goole Moors, is apparent from this view recorded in the 1950s. An ex-NER slotted signal can be seen, still in use, on the right as a steam-hauled freight comprising a single goods van (but apparently requiring two brake vans!) heads off on the 5½-mile branch to Fockerby. *D. Lawrence*

Right: Ivatt Class 2 2-6-0 No 46407 with a couple of brake vans at Reedness Junction on 22 July 1961. Although by its very nature seasonal, agricultural produce continued to provide traffic for the line until April 1965. *Hugh Davis*

Above: The daily freight at Fockerby on 22 July 1961. This was (and remains) a productive agricultural area, notable for potatoes but in parts also for peat. At one time the Fockerby branch also generated as much as a third of the joint railway's total passenger revenue, but by the time of its withdrawal, in July 1933, the service had dwindled to a single train per day in each direction.
Hugh Davis

Left: Ivatt Class 2 2-6-0 No 46478 at the buffer-stops at Fockerby on 22 July 1961. Locomotives such as this provided the bulk of services in the 1950s and early 1960s and were provided mainly by Goole shed (50D). The wooden station office seen here has since been removed, but that at Eastoft survives.
Hugh Davis

Above: The enamel BR sign at the entrance to Fockerby goods depot, seen from Station Road on 22 July 1961. The facilities here, which at one time included a passenger station, were located some distance from the village they purported to serve. *Hugh Davis*

STATION ROAD FOCKERBY

Right: The same location on 15 August 2008. Although the station yard has been replaced by agricultural buildings, the stationmaster's house remains extant in private ownership. *Author*

Right: The Isle of Axholme is surrounded by the rivers Trent, Don and Idle, but access by rail required a single-track viaduct over the River Torne and Folley Drain. Photographed on 15 August 2008, this was the most distinctive engineering structure on the joint line, having two large arches over the main waterways and six smaller arches. The crown of each arch was numbered with a cast-iron plate. *Author*

South Yorkshire

The 20-mile South Yorkshire Joint Railway was at one time owned jointly by no fewer than five railway companies — the Midland, GCR, GNR, LYR and NER — and is today the principal survivor of four inter-connected joint ventures in the South Yorkshire Coalfield. Prior to the 1923 Grouping this was served by six major railways, but the impracticality of their providing competing lines in the area brought the rivals together to form a number of joint railways.

Of those that are closed, the GC, H&B & Midland Joint commenced operations in 1910 and ran from Anston Junction to Braithwell Junction, where it divided. From 1909 the 4½-mile GC & Midland Joint ran west to the Rotherham–Swinton lines of both the LYR and GCR, and in May 1916 the H&B & GC

Joint was opened, running some 25½ miles north from Braithwell Junction to Aire Junction, on the H&B line. Although this line provided a goods depot at Doncaster York Road, it also acted as a freight 'bypass' for the town. The mineral line was never used by regular passenger services, as these would have interfered with the business of moving coal.

Although the main section of the former South Yorkshire Joint Railway and a short stretch of the GC & Midland Joint at Dinnington remain open in 2010, they lost their regular passenger services in 1929. The freight-only line to Firbeck Colliery was lifted in 1970, while the other joint lines all closed along with the collieries and industries they served. The GC, H&B & Midland Joint lost its through traffic in 1966, but the Anston Junction–Thurcroft Colliery section remained until January 1992, and the western section of the GC & Midland Joint, to Silverwood Colliery, survived until June 1996, the final use of this remaining section being to remove the colliery stockpile. The northern section of the H&B & GC Joint closed to through traffic in 1950, although parts were used subsequently for wagon storage. The Aire Junction– Bullcroft Junction section closed in October 1958, while all use of the remaining southern section from Braithwell Junction had ceased by September 1970. Whereas there has been extensive landscaping upon closure of the collieries, many of the bridges survive, and traces of all the joint lines remain.

Above: In later years many of the original cast-iron bridge numberplates were replaced by stencilled numbers, as seen on 14 August 2008 on this road bridge (RB) carrying the former Midland, GC & H&B Joint Railway over a country lane at Thurcroft. This area, southwest of Maltby, was heavily landscaped following closure of Thurcroft Colliery on 31 January 1992, and nowadays the line that once served the pit is difficult to trace for much of its route. *Author*

Above: An excursion to Cleethorpes, headed by ex-NER Class B16/1 4-6-0 No 61429, threads its way slowly over the Pontefract Loop, between Pontefract Monkhill and Pontefract Baghill, on the erstwhile Swinton & Knottingley Joint Railway (NER/MR). As can be seen, one of the two tracks had already been lifted by the time the photograph was taken, on 31 July 1957. The loop closed in November 1964, but most of the remainder of the former joint line remains open. *P. Cookson*

Centre right: Brush Type 4 No D1784 at Markham Main Colliery, near Doncaster, on 1 March 1967. This was one of eight collieries on the former South Yorkshire Joint Railway, coal being the reason for all the joint railways in this area. Along with the pit the spur from the main line is now closed, but the majority of the old South Yorkshire Joint Railway remains open in 2010, serving the two remaining collieries. *D. Colley*

Right: The GC & H&B Joint Railway was constructed on reasonably flat country north of Doncaster. The route is identifiable today by the many rusting metal-girder road bridges over the disused line, this example being photographed at Sykehouse on 14 August 2008. More than 40 similar bridges of blue-engineering-brick-and-steel-girder construction were erected on the Braithwell–Thorpe-in-Balne section. *Author*

West Yorkshire

The Methley Joint Railway was opened for freight in June 1865 by the LYR, GNR and NER. Just 5 miles in length, it connected the GNR's Wakefield–Leeds main line with the NER at Castleford. Passenger services, between Castleford, Leeds and Wakefield and operated by the GNR, began in June 1869, and there were two intermediate stations, at Methley and Stanley. Throughout its existence the railway suffered flooding at its eastern end, being built on the flood plain of the River Calder, while mining subsidence also caused problems on parts of the line. The line closed to local passenger services in March 1960 and as a through freight route in November 1964, a surviving stub following in April 1967. The joint station at Methley survives, but that at Stanley has been demolished.

The Halifax High Level & North & South Junction Railway was a grandly titled railway that ran just 3 miles from Homefield to Halifax St Pauls. Opened in September 1890, it climbed some 300ft above the town and was known simply as the Halifax High Level. The adjoining Halifax & Ovenden Junction Railway had opened its 2½-mile line as a freight link in September 1874 and to passengers in December 1879. Both concerns were owned jointly by the GNR and LYR and gave improved access to Halifax for the GNR, which worked the services. Passenger services on the High Level line were withdrawn in January 1917 but continued on the H&O line until May 1955; goods traffic on both lines ceased in July 1960.

Elsewhere in West Yorkshire the Otley & Ilkley Joint Railway provided a 3-mile spur linking the two towns and was a collaborative venture between the Midland and North Eastern railways. Opened to passengers in August 1865 and to freight the following year, it closed in March 1965.

For completeness, mention should also be made of Leeds Central station, owned jointly by the GNR, LNWR, LYR and NER. Closed in April 1967, it is described more fully in *Lost Lines: North Eastern*.

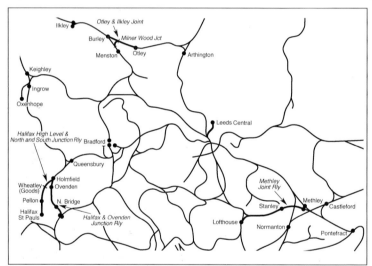

Below left: Methley South station, on the erstwhile Methley Joint Railway (GN, LY & NE), in the early 1950s, with ex-GER Class N7 0-6-2T No 69695, fitted with a higher bunker, arriving with a two-coach local train. The line remained a joint (LMS/LNER) route after the Grouping, and the station continued to be known as Methley Joint until renamed by BR as Methley South. *D. Lawrence*

Below: The Methley Joint Railway was distinctive in the design of its stations, and even the uniforms were issued with specially inscribed buttons. The former stationmaster's house at Methley South still survives, and traces of BR Eastern Region green paint could still be seen when this photograph was taken on 15 August 2008. *Author's collection*

Above: Stanley station on the one-time Methley Joint Railway, with ex-GNR Class N1 0-6-2T No 69430 arriving at the platform. The locomotive, the first of its class, was withdrawn in December 1956, giving a clue to the date of the photograph. The station, the sign and gas lamps here lending it a distinct GNR ambience, has since been completely obliterated. *D. Lawrence*

Above: Leeds Central station was originally the joint property of the GNR, LNWR, LYR and NER. This atmospheric view with, on the right, an ex-GCR Class N5 0-6-2T in BR livery and, taking water on the left, an ex-GNR Class C12 4-4-2T still in LNER livery, was recorded in the summer of 1948. Nationalisation at the start of the year had brought an end to the station's joint (latterly LNER/LMS) status. *Ian Allan Library*

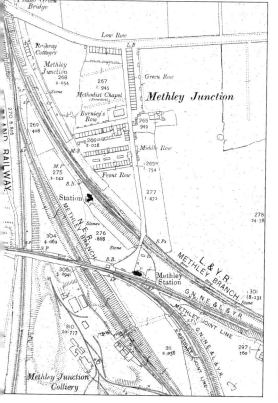

Above: Ex-LMS Fairburn Class 4 2-6-4T No 42699 on pilot duty at Leeds Central station in April 1967, just a few days before closure of this by now rather dirty and run-down terminus. The station would be demolished after closure. A full history appears in *Lost Lines: North Eastern. Ian Allan Library*

Left: Methley stations and lines in 1905. The joint-line station buildings are to the south of the map, the station house and access bridge, over the closed LYR branch, survives in 2010. *Crown copyright*

21 Cheshire Lines Committee and joint connections

This was the second-largest joint railway, with some 143 miles of line. Its title was slightly misleading in that, while the railway was formed to regulate traffic on proposed lines in Cheshire, most of it was eventually situated in Lancashire. Nevertheless, with its smartly timed express trains and heavy freight flows the CLC could once have laid claim to being the premier joint railway.

Formed in 1865 to administer a number of local lines, the Committee consisted originally of directors from the Manchester, Sheffield & Lincoln (later to become the Great Central) and Great Northern railways, and these were joined in 1866 by representatives of the Midland. All three railways used the CLC to try to break the monopoly of the LNWR in the North West, but the CLC developed a distinctive style for its stations, passenger stock and goods depots that belied allegiance to the constituent companies. However, whilst it possessed its own rolling stock (including four Sentinel steam railcars) the CLC never had its own locomotives. As the joint arrangements were established relatively early, they were sometimes used as a guide for the running of other joint lines.

Of the lost CLC routes perhaps the most significant was a heavily used freight line from Glazebrook, bypassing Manchester via Stockport to the south, which afforded direct contact with the MR at Cheadle and to the GCR's Sheffield line at Godley Junction. Branches from the Chester Northgate line ran to Winsford & Over and to Helsby, where a connection was made with the Birkenhead Joint Railway. There were also large-scale freight operations at Manchester, Liverpool and Birkenhead, including the docks and a monopoly of freight to the Trafford Park Estate at Manchester.

Although the CLC incorporated several existing railways, it was responsible for construction of the Winsford & Over branch, open to all traffic by July 1870, and the Glazebrook–Skelton Junction line, opened in March 1873 (and realigned in 1893 near Cadishead, where the railway was required to span the newly opened Manchester Ship Canal). March 1874 saw the opening of Liverpool Central station, which became the CLC's headquarters. Services on the link to Chester Northgate station began in the same year, while the Romily–Stockport line opened in 1875.

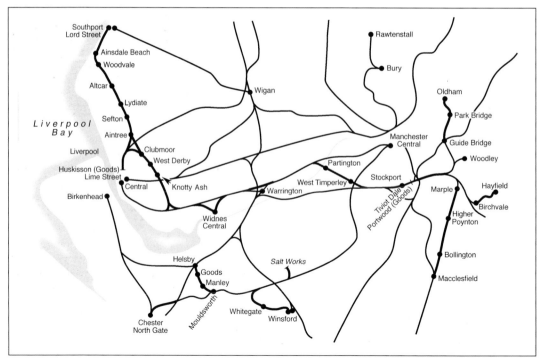

Above: Manchester Central station, by now missing numerous panes of glass, on 22 August 1962. The CLC's plans to build an office and hotel directly adjoining the station frontage never came to fruition, but a covered walkway once led to the nearby Midland Hotel. Opened in July 1880, the terminus had an arched trainshed measuring 210ft (64m) across, and at its peak in the early 20th century its nine platforms handled about 400 trains daily. The largest CLC station to have been lost, it survives in use as a conference and exhibition centre. *H. Bowtell*

Right: CLC garter crest incorporating the heraldic shields of its owners, the Great Northern (top), Great Central (bottom left) and Midland railways.

Manchester Central station opened in July 1880, while the line to Liverpool Docks at Huskisson and the link to Aintree also opened during that year.

A number of other closed joint railways were once linked to the CLC. One operated by the CLC itself was the Southport & Cheshire Lines Extension Railway, which extended the CLC from Aintree to Southport; this line, together with associated CLC routes around Liverpool and those of the Birkenhead Joint Railway, are included in *Lost Lines: Liverpool and the Mersey*. A separate entity, the Sheffield & Midland Railways Joint Committee, which in 1904 became the GC & Midland Railways Joint Committee, provided a branch to Hayfield and constructed a loop from the CLC Liverpool–Manchester main line to serve Widnes Central. There was also the Macclesfield Committee; this became the GC&NS Joint Railway in 1908 and

operated the line from Macclesfield, on the North Staffordshire Railway, through Bollington to join the CLC near Marple. Further north was the Oldham, Ashton-under-Lyne & Guide Bridge Junction Railway, a joint LNWR/GCR line that had opened in 1861.

Upon creation of the 'Big Four' railway companies in 1923 the CLC remained a separate joint entity, as it was feared that allocation to either the LNER or LMS might disadvantage the other. The LNER, with five directors and controlling two thirds of the CLC, provided the majority of the motive power, while the LMS, with two directors, was responsible for the permanent way; an eighth, independent director was also appointed. The CLC finally succumbed upon nationalisation of the railways in 1948, but even then carriages lettered 'CLC' were produced by BR for a while.

Of the CLC routes that have closed, the line to Huskisson Dock lost its passenger service as long ago as 1885 but remained open for freight until 1976. Meanwhile the Winsford & Over branch closed to passengers in January 1931 and to freight in June 1967. July 1981 saw closure of the line between Godley Junction and Apethorne Junction, and August 1982 the Partington–Glazebrook section over the Manchester Ship Canal, while use of the singled line from Partington to Skelton Junction ceased in 1994. Freight on the Cheadle Heath–Stockport Tiviot Dale–Bredbury section lasted until 1982, and the Mouldsworth–Helsby line closed to all remaining traffic in September 1991.

Of the joint lines that adjoined the CLC the link to Southport closed in January 1952, and the loop to Widnes Central in October 1964. May 1967 witnessed the closure of the OAGB link, while the New Mills–Hayfield line succumbed in January 1970, as did the Rose Hill (Marple)–Macclesfield line.

Most of the large CLC stations have closed to passengers — Stockport Tiviot Dale in January 1967, Manchester Central and Chester Northgate in October 1969 and Liverpool Central in April 1972. Sadly all but Manchester Central have been demolished. All the CLC freight depots have also closed. The large facility alongside Central station in Manchester and those in Liverpool have been demolished, but former CLC warehouses survive in alternative use at Birkenhead and Warrington.

In spite of all the closures a good deal of the erstwhile CLC remains open. Many of its distinctive country stations also survive, while the former Manchester Central is now used as an exhibition and conference centre.

Above: Liverpool Central on 24 October 1964 — a far cry from the days when this was the headquarters of the CLC. The station closed in April 1972, the elegant trainshed, some 65ft (19.8m) high, being demolished shortly afterwards, but the site remains identifiable in 2010. *J. Clarke*

Below: Stockport Tiviot Dale (originally Teviot Dale), with its unique frontage of 30 arches, seen in August 1964. The Jacobean-styled station was opened in 1865 by the Stockport, Timperley & Altrincham Junction Railway, which by amalgamation was destined to form part of the CLC, in 1867. The station was demolished after closure to passengers in January 1967. *J. Clarke*

Right: Stockport Tiviot Dale on 2 July 1963, with ex-LMS Class 4F 0-6-0 No 44250 shunting coaching stock. Your author used this station in April 1965, expecting Tiviot Dale to be a rural area rather than in the town centre! Freight trains continued to run through until 1982, when damage was caused by the construction of the nearby M63. The track was lifted in 1986, and today no trace remains of the station. *L. Sandler*

Right: Cast-iron CLC sign.

Below: Departures from Stockport Tiviot Dale, April 1956.

Below right: A DMU train from New Brighton after arrival at Chester Northgate on 6 August 1967. The station opened in November 1874, its two trainsheds the least grand of the CLC's main termini. Closure in October 1969 was followed by demolition, and the site has since been redeveloped. *Author*

TIVIOT DALE STATION.

From St. Pancras via Chinley.
1st cl.—Single 43/2, Return 86/4.
3rd cl.—Single 28/9, Return 57/6.

St. Pan.	Stock.	Stock.	St. Pan.
a.m.		a.m.	
8 15er	1 22	12‡20c	6 54
8 15s	1 25	8 51r	2 1
10 15er	3 1	p.m.	
p.m.		1 35er	6 14
2 15r	6‡19	1 35s	6 19
4 15r	8 57	—	—
6 40r	11 14	—	—
Sunday Trains.			
p.m.		a.m.	
3 30	8 42	12 25	6 30
6 10r	10 53	8 55r	3 0
—	—	p.m.	
—	—	1 48	7 20
—	—	5 36	11 30

‡ Cheadle Heath Station.
c Not Monday. e Not Saturday.
r Refreshment Car.
s Saturday only.

Above: Diverted on account of track re-laying between Hyde Junction and Godley, the 8.40am Manchester–Sheffield DMU train is seen on the CLC route from Apethorne Junction to Godley Junction, having left the direct route at Hyde Junction and reversed at Woodley. The photograph was taken on Sunday 13 September 1964. *J. Clarke*

Left: Passing a distinctive CLC signal, Stanier Class 5 2-6-0 No 42975 pounds up the steep gradient from Portwood, near Tiviot Dale, and approaches Bredbury Junction with a freight for Dewsnap Sidings on a cold afternoon in February 1956. The steep climb eastward from Stockport meant that freight trains often required banking on this section of line. The trackbed here is now used as a footpath and cycleway. *J. Hillier*

Above: Winsford & Over was the terminus of the branch from Cuddington. The line served a salt works, and the station nameboard remained *in situ* long after the withdrawal of regular passenger services, in January 1931. Here ex-GCR Class C13 4-4-2T No 67436 is seen calling with an RCTS special in October 1953. Note the clerestory coach leading. *Ian Allan Library*

Right: Class 45/1 No 45 120 heads Hertfordshire Railtours' 'Olive Branch' special past the former Helsby & Alvanley station, on the Mouldsworth–West Cheshire Junction section of the erstwhile CLC, on 14 March 1987. Although regular passenger services had ceased in 1944 freight traffic continued, this section of former joint line closing only in September 1991. *G. Smith*

Above left: Destined to be the last of its class in service, ex-GCR 'C14' 4-4-2T No 67450 leaves Hayfield with the 5.35pm train to Manchester London Road via Reddish on 15 June 1957. This single-line outer-suburban branch was worked originally by the Sheffield & Midland Railways Joint Committee. *B. Green*

Left: On 9 April 1969 the 12.56pm from Manchester to Macclesfield via Hyde enters Higher Poynton, on the 10½-mile former GC & NS Joint Railway. Opened as the Macclesfield, Bollington & Marple Railway, this linked the GCR and NSR and became a joint concern in 1871. Passenger services were of a local nature, and the line closed in January 1970, to become a footpath for most of its length. *I. Smith*

Above left: CLC mileage posts were tall, distinctive and marked with the committee's initials. This example was photographed in July 2009 at Winchcombe Railway Museum. *Author*

Top: The 168yd (154m) Brinnington No 2 Tunnel, just east of Brinnington Junction (itself east of Stockport Tiviot Dale), was built on both a curve and a rising gradient. The trackbed here is used nowadays as a footpath and cycleway; this photograph was taken on 23 July 2009. *Author*

Above: The large former CLC warehouse at Birkenhead survives, albeit in office and other usage, this photograph dating from September 2006. Freight to and from this facility travelled over the Birkenhead Joint Railway (LMS & GWR Joint), the closed sections of which, along with Birkenhead Woodside station, are described in *Lost Lines: Liverpool and the Mersey*. *Author*

22 Preston & Wyre Joint Railway

In the early 19th century Wyre Dock and Fleetwood became particularly important for trade with Ireland, while Blackpool developed to become the premier holiday resort in the North of England, at one time being responsible for the country's greatest seasonal flow of traffic. Thus it was that in 1849 the LNWR and LYR joined forces to run the 46 miles of line (and docks) of the Preston & Wyre Railway Harbour & Dock Co, which they leased in the proportion of two thirds to the LNWR and one third to the LYR. Nevertheless, the railway continued to be operated as a separate entity until 1888, when it was vested in the LNWR and LYR and its shareholders received shares of both these railways.

The line to Blackpool split at Kirkham, one route running to Blackpool North, together with a line to Wyre Dock and Fleetwood, the other to Waterloo Road and Blackpool Central, via Lytham. The direct Kirkham–Waterloo Road line was built in 1903 to relieve congestion during peak holiday periods.

Interestingly the joint status of this line ended with the amalgamation of the LNWR and LYR in 1922 when the railway became entirely the property of the LNWR, which in turn became part of the LMS the following year.

Just as the railway originally had an immense influence on the growth of Blackpool, social and economic changes after World War 2 saw a decline in

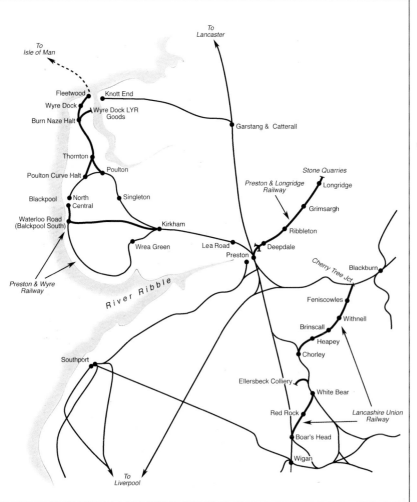

Right: Extensive sidings were provided south of Blackpool Central station and are recorded here in 1933. Between the 1890s and 1930s the sidings were doubled in capacity. Today the former sidings have been turned into car parking areas and roads. *Crown copyright*

Right: Blackpool Central station frontage, dating from 1900, with taxis waiting under an iron-and-glass *porte cochère* in the 1950s. The station was, as its name suggests, well sited in the centre of Blackpool and close to the sandy beach. 'Wakes Week' saw complete towns close down and their population depart *en masse* to Blackpool, requiring the station here to deal with huge crowds of holidaymakers. *D. Lawrence*

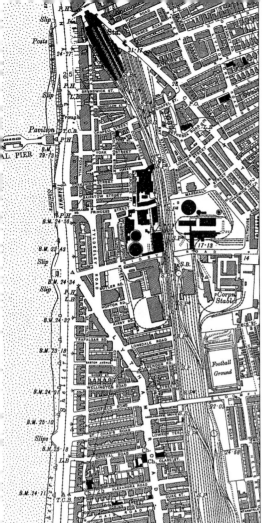

British coastal resorts and use of the lines. Several big functional Victorian structures were a feature of the line, but by the mid-1960s a loss of glass in Blackpool North station's roof and the reduction of tracks from four to two added to the gloom that was apparent by that time.

Blackpool Central and the link to it closed in November 1964. The direct line from Kirkham, via Marton, to Blackpool South, closed in February 1967 and has been converted into a road. Passenger services to Fleetwood, that had been curtailed to a new platform at Wyre Dock, ceased in June 1970 (see *Lost Lines: LMR*). Blackpool tram services still connect close to the sites of the closed stations, while passenger trains may yet return to Fleetwood.

LNWR / LYR joint railways

Also to be found in this part of Lancashire were various other railways owned jointly by the LNWR and LYR. The Preston & Longridge Railway, a 6¾-mile branch north-east from Preston station, opened in 1840 and until 1848 was worked by horses. The LYR and LNWR assumed ownership in 1867, the line's joint status ending upon their amalgamation in 1922. Passenger services were withdrawn in June 1930, but goods traffic continued until November 1967, and a southern section to a Courtaulds siding survived until February 1980.

The Wigan–Blackburn route relied on the use of two sections of the Lancashire Union Railway, which became a joint venture between the LYR and LNWR. Passenger services between Chorley and Blackburn were withdrawn in January 1960 and freight in April 1968, the remaining southern section of this line, between Boar's Head and White Bear, closing in December 1971.

Left: Blackpool Central in the late 1950s, with two ex-LYR locomotives in use as stationary boilers for heating carriages. Nearer the camera is ex-LYR 0-4-4T No 613, dating from 1878 and withdrawn in 1910. Beyond the locomotives is the station toilet, which survived until June 2009. *D. Lawrence*

Centre left: Blackpool Central closed in November 1964 and is seen here after all the tracks had been filled in up to platform level and the area was in use as car park. When this view was taken on 24 June 1965, the station buildings were being converted to a bingo hall. The station, with its clock and offices, was subsequently demolished. *R. Fisher*

Below left: Blackpool Central was built on an elevated site, and much of the retaining wall survives, although the section seen here (on 3 July 2009) has suffered from subsidence. Excursion traffic to Blackpool was once considerable: on August Bank Holiday 1910, for example, almost 100 trains and 48,000 passengers used Blackpool Central station. By 2009 the station site was used as a car park, but rail excursions still run to Blackpool North. *Author*

Below: Lengthy bridges were required under (or over) the mass of lines than ran south from Blackpool Central, and three of these survive. This photograph of the Rigby Road underbridge, its walls lined with white glazed bricks to give added light for pedestrians, was taken on 3 July 2009. *Author*

Right: At one time there were connecting sailings from Fleetwood to Ireland and the Isle of Man, and a local rail service ran direct to Blackpool, but by the time this photograph was taken on 1 August 1964 — a Bank Holiday — the station was under threat of closure, and the glass in the iron roof of the imposing 1883 structure had already been removed. The run-down station finally closed in April 1966 and was subsequently demolished, but the possibility of restoring passenger services to Fleetwood should not be discounted. *J. Woods*

Centre right: Ex-LMS Stanier Class 8F 2-8-0 No 48739 shunting at Longridge with the 11.30am goods from Lostock Hall on 26 August 1966. This former joint (LYR/LNWR) branch had closed to passengers in June 1930, but a cotton mill and quarries beyond the station continued to freight traffic until October 1967, and a southern section from Preston to a Courtaulds siding survived until February 1980. *L. Sandler*

Below: Rest in peace. Looking not unlike a tombstone, this early stone boundary marker of the LYR & LNW Joint Railways was photographed at Winchcombe Railway Museum in July 2009. *Author*

Below right: The Preston Park Hotel opened in 1882 and was designed by Arnold Mitchell. The red-brick building was located in a commanding position overlooking the River Ribble at Preston but also close to the station. Construction costs were contributed jointly by the LYR and LNWR, although the hotel was administered by the latter's Hotel Committee on behalf of the LYR. The property was sold out of railway ownership in 1949, but in 2010 the building remained in use with Lancashire County Council. *Author*

23 Whitehaven, Cleator & Egremont Railway

Beneath the wind-lashed moors of West Cumbria lay deposits of coal, limestone and haematite iron ore, and in 1842 an iron works opened at Cleator Moor. Cleator grew with the Industrial Revolution, and from the late 1840s the area became known as 'Little Ireland', reflecting the number of migrants displaced by the Irish potato famine. Founded near Parton was the Lowca Engineering Works, succeeded in 1857 by Fletcher Jennings, the locomotive builder, while at Workington steel rails were produced.

West Cumbria thus became an industrialised area, and the Whitehaven, Cleator & Egremont Railway was spawned to serve its quarries, ironworks and mines and provide a link to the coast. The Whitehaven (Mirehouse Junction)–Moor Row–Egremont section opened for freight in January 1857, a line to Frizington opening at the same time. Extensions from Frizington to Eskett and Rowrah had been completed by November 1862, and the northern section from Rowrah to Marron Junction, providing a link with the LNWR's Workington line, opened in January 1866. South from Egremont a connection with the Furness Railway at Sellafield opened in August 1869, while a branch from Ullock Junction to Distington opened in 1879 and was extended to Parton in 1881.

The Corkicle–Rowrah and Woodend–Egremont sections were the first of a number of sections provided with double track, as iron-ore traffic increased. Deviations were sometimes required to deal with mining subsidence, and many new sidings and links were opened to colliery and iron-ore workings. By 1881 some 35 miles of main route were provided, and, although the area remained sparsely populated, local passenger services were also introduced.

When plans for a link from Egremont to the coast were proposed the Whitehaven & Furness Junction Railway (WFJR) objected, being concerned that this would reduce traffic on its own coastal route. The LNWR was also keen to absorb the busy WCE. This all provided impetus for greater co-operation in the area, and proposals were put forward for joint ownership of the WCE. As it turned out the Furness Railway had taken over the WFJR before the new line was built and had shares in the WCE. The LNWR also had shares in the WCE, and consequently in 1878 the WCE was acquired jointly by the Furness and the LNWR railways, although 'joint' was not added to the title.

The hitherto joint line became wholly owned by the LMS in 1923, by which time the line to Parton, which had lost its intermittent passenger service in 1914, had closed to all traffic (in 1922). Regular services over the Moor Row–Marron Junction section ceased in April 1931, the Whitehaven–Moor Row–Sellafield service likewise in January 1935, although excursion trains to Morecambe and other holiday destinations continued to run. Passenger services on the Whitehaven–Moor Row–Sellafield section were briefly revived in 1946/7, and workmen's trains between Moor Row and Sellafield continued until 1964. Meanwhile the

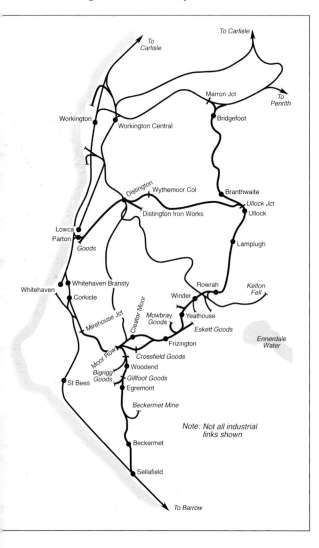

northern Rowrah–Marron Junction section had closed to remaining freight traffic in May 1954. Other lines lasted longer, and the Beckermet–Sellafield section, at one time regarded as a strategic evacuation route in the event of a nuclear accident at Sellafield, survived until January 1970. Closure in 1978 of the haematite quarry at Rowrah led to this section's being taken out of use in February of that year, and the line was lifted in 1980. In October of that year the mine at Beckermet also closed, ultimately leading to the withdrawal in September 1982 of all services over the surviving line to Mirehouse Junction via Moor Row.

Today the entire network of lines has been lifted, but many stone-built stations and bridges remain, while sections of the trackbed form part of the long-distance cycleway from St Bees to Robin Hood's Bay.

Right: LMS Class 3F 0-6-2T No 11638, formerly Furness Railway No 109, at Moor Row shed on 2 July 1932. These locomotives were gradually withdrawn after the joint FR/LNWR line became wholly LMS property at the Grouping. Moor Row shed, focus of the line's goods activities, survived into BR days, eventually closing in July 1954. *H. C. Casserley*

Right: Ex-LMS Ivatt Class 4MT 2-6-0 No 43004 enters Cleator Moor station with the 2.10pm Rowrah Quarry–Moor Row freight on 7 May 1963. The goods yard was still busy at this time, and on the right of the picture a local coal merchant can be seen loading sacks of coal on to his lorry. Today the remains of one of the stone-built goods platforms can still be found amongst the undergrowth at this location. *N. Machell*

Right: Class 3F 0-6-0 No 52501 at Moor Row station with the 'West Cumberland Rail Tour' of 5 September 1954. Originally FR No 20, the locomotive was one of a series of 19 designed by Pettigrew and built between 1913 and 1920. Although regular passenger services had been withdrawn in January 1935, the station nameboards (and the sign for the gents' toilets) remained *in situ* at Moor Row, which at this time was still used by workmen's trains and special excursions. *Ian Allan Library*

Left: Another view featuring the 'West Cumberland Rail Tour' of 5 September 1954, still with No 52501 in charge, this time at Rowrah. Note that the platform on the right is edged with stone, while that on the left, added when the line here was doubled, is edged with wood. When iron-ore mining was at is height a mineral railway ran to the east of the station to serve local haematite mines. *Ian Allan Library*

Left: The same train photographed at Distington, with Distington Joint signalbox on the right. Distington was once a junction on the WCE Ullock Junction–Parton line. The iron works here closed in 1922, and the WCE line soon after, but freight services on an alternative route to Distington survived until June 1964. The buildings have since been demolished, and the area has been returned to agricultural use. *Ian Allan Library*

Left: Passing through Egremont on 10 September 1980, Class 25/3 No 25 292 heads a mineral train from the Beckermet haematite mine to the steelworks at Workington, once famous for its production of steel rails. Workings at the mine had ceased some while previously, and the last section of the former joint line closed in October 1980, since when part of the trackbed at Egremont has been used as the basis of a road. *Dr J. McGregor*

Above left: The stone-built stations and goods sheds on the WCE showed a clear FR influence, as apparent from this photograph of the station at Rowrah, taken on 2 July 2009. Similar station buildings survive at Woodend and Beckermet, the former including the remains of a FR/LNWR Joint Railway platform wall clock, while at Beckermet is an original lamp-post. *Author*

Above: Moor Row on 2 July 2009. Although the station buildings have been demolished, much of the extensive site once occupied by the railway has remained derelict since final closure of the line in 1980, and one lengthy platform remains. The trackbed is now used as part of the long-distance Coast-to-Coast footpath/cycleway from St Bees to Robin Hood's Bay. *Author*

Right: At one time connected to the WCE at Egremont, Florence No 2 Mine was the last deep haematite mine in Western Europe. This view of the mine, which is now a heritage centre, was recorded on 2 July 2009. The ex-BR wagons, dating from 1951, came from Workington and serve a reminder of the area's busy network of industrial railways. *Author*

24

Portpatrick & Wigtownshire Joint Railway

The short (22-mile) sea passage between Portpatrick and Donaghadee was recognised by Victorian railways as providing a speedy route to Ireland for passengers and mail, and the Portpatrick Railway's main line westwards from Castle Douglas, on the Glasgow & South Western Railway, to Stranraer opened in March 1861, being extended to Portpatrick itself in August 1862. The Newton Stewart–Whithorn and Millisle–Garlieston branches were opened throughout in July 1877 by the Wigtownshire Railway, which employed as its engineer Thomas Bouch, who was also responsible for the ill-fated Tay Bridge.

The rugged nature of this remote part of Scotland required considerable engineering works, most notably the viaduct spanning the Big Water of Fleet, and made these expensive lines to construct. Furthermore, a delay in implementing the Admiralty's plans to improve the harbour at Portpatrick created problems in transporting mail from that port (the 'Irish Mail' from Holyhead being already established), and the opening of the Glasgow–Stranraer line exacerbated the financial problems of the Portpatrick and Wigtownshire railways. As a consequence the lines of both companies were purchased jointly in 1885 by the London & North Western, Midland, Caledonian and Glasgow & South Western railways, being operated thereafter as the Portpatrick & Wigtownshire Joint Railway. Although the 82¼-mile joint line used locomotives and rolling stock (hired at mileage rates)

from the CR and GSWR it thus became the only significant line in Scotland at that time to be owned, at least in part, by English railways.

Stranraer was always seen as the port for heavy goods and soon developed as a favourable alternative to Portpatrick for all traffic. Frequent steamer services to Larne were introduced, and, besides the Irish cattle trade, the port became important for the Royal Mail service to Northern Ireland. The line became known as the 'Port Road', as boat trains and through sleeping cars to and from London provided important connecting ferry traffic.

Garlieston was the nearest port to the Isle of Man, and excursions to Douglas were introduced. As the harbour was tidal regular sailings could not be provided, but it nevertheless generated some tourist traffic along the line.

Joint ownership ended at the 1923 Grouping, when the constituent companies were merged to form the LMS. The line was very busy during World War 2, and a new port was opened by the LMS at Cairnryan, although, as related in *Lost Lines: Scotland*, this was destined to close after the war.

The railway operated in a remote and sparsely populated area of Scotland, and this led to a number of early closures. The 1-in-35 gradient link to the pier at Portpatrick was difficult to operate and was abandoned as early as 1874. Regular passenger services on the line to Garlieston were withdrawn in March 1903, although excursions continued until 1935, and freight

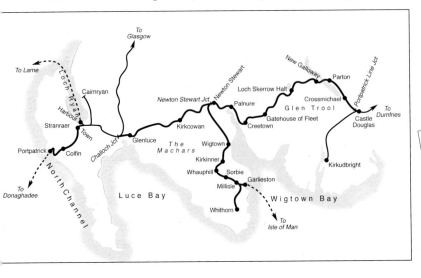

Above right: Portpatrick in 1907, showing the harbour branch that required reversal at the main terminus. *Crown copyright*

Right: Portpatrick & Wigtownshire Joint Railway timetable, April 1910.

EXPRESS SERVICES
between
LONDON and
BELFAST
Via STRANRAER AND LARNE

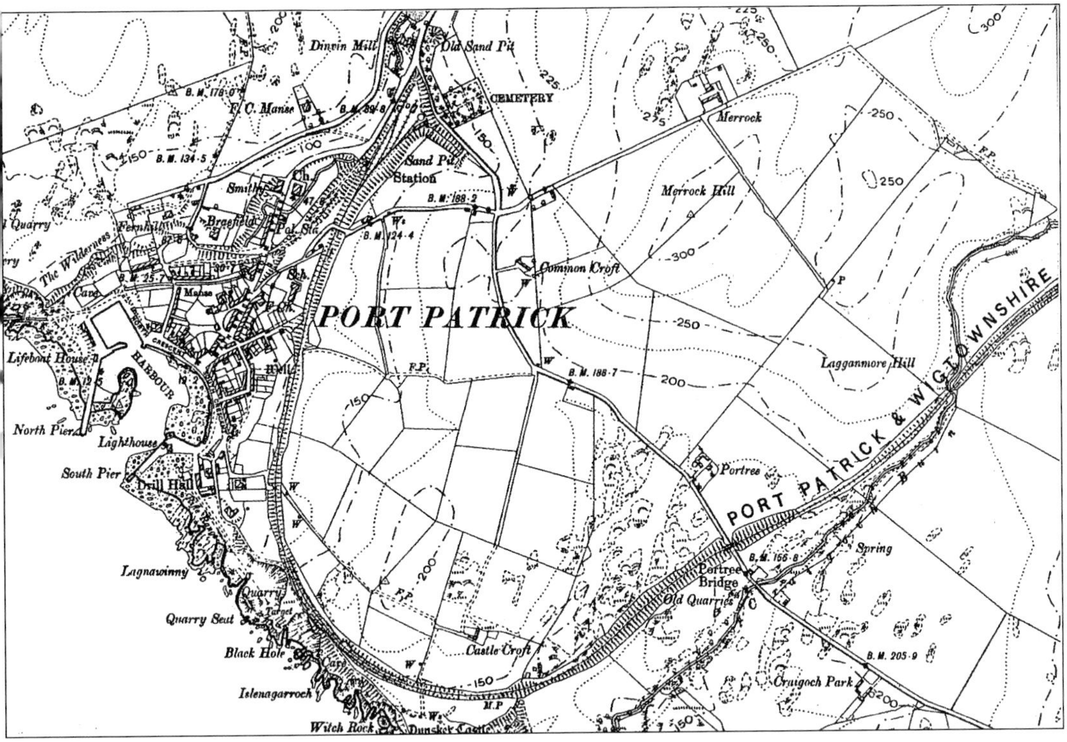

Traff. Man. and Sec., Fred. W. Hutchinson.] **PORTPATRICK and WIGTOWNSHIRE JOINT.**

Miles from Castle Douglas.	**Down.**	Week Days. aft	mrn	mrn	mrn	aft	aft	mrn	mrn
	London								
	830 Euston .... dep.	8b0	...	...	...	1150	...	5 0	10 0
	830 St. Pancras .... "	8q15	...	...	...	12 0	...	5 0	9 30
	404 B'mingham (N.St., LNW) "	8b40	...	...	...	11r0	...	7 20	1115
	579 " (" Mid.). "	7z18	...	...	...	1125	...	3k55	1025
	830 Liverpool (Lime Street) "	10b55	...	...	...	1245	...	9 50	1110
	830 " (Exchange)* .. "	...	...	...	...	2 30	...	9 47	1250
	830 Manchester (Exchange) "	11b0	...	...	...	1 0	...	9 20	11 5
	758 " (Victoria)* "	...	...	...	...	...	...	9 50	1240
	610 Leeds (Wellington) ..... "	12 38	...	...	...	4 8	...	10 0	1 33
	830 Liverpool (Exchange) † "	...	...	...	...	1245	...	9 25	1235
	830 Manchester (Victoria) † "	...	...	...	...	1250	...	9 32	1230
	684 York (N.E.) .... "	10o30	...	...	...	...	...	7 40	9 57
	696 Newcastle (Central) .... "	d 10	...	...	...	...	...	1020	1 18
	830 Carlisle (Cit., G.&S.W.) "	3 10	...	...	...	7 0	...	1 30	4 2
	855 Edinbro' (Princes St.) ... "	...	...	...	...	...	...	1010	2 5
	855 Glasgow (Central) .... "	...	...	...	...	...	...	1020	2 5
	831 " (St. Enoch) .. "	9 30	...	...	...	...	...	1110	2 30
	885 Lockerbie .... "	mrn	...	...	...	7 35	...	1 30	4 45
	839 Dumfries .... "	3 55	...	...	...	8 30	...	2 50	6 0
—	**Castle Douglas** .... dep	4 26	...	...	...	9 25	Fridays only.	3 30	6 39
3¼	Crossmichael	...	...	...	...	9 33		3 37	6 46
6¾	Parton.	...	...	...	...	9 40		3 44	6 52
8¾	New Galloway	...	...	...	...	9 46		3 50	6 58
18¾	Dromore.	...	...	...	...	10 8		4 12	7 17
23½	Creetown	...	...	...	...	1020		4 24	7 27
26½	Palnure.	...	...	...	...	1025		4 29	7 32
29¾	**Newton-Stewart** .... arr.	5 8	...	...	...	1031		4 35	7 39
—	**Newton-Stewart** .... dep.	6 15	...	8 30	Fridays only.	1053	2 30	5 0	8 10
36¾	Wigtown	6 31	...	8 51		11 9	2 45	5 16	8 29
39	Kirkinner	6 37	...	9 0		1115	2 51	5 22	8 36
40¾	Whauphill	6 43	...	9 10		1121	2 57	5 28	8 42
43¾	Sorbie	6 49	...	9 20		1127	3 3	5 34	8 49
45	Millisle, for Garlieston ...	6 55	...	9 32		1133	3 8	5 40	8 55
49	**Whithorn** .... arr.	7 5	...	9 42		1143	3 18	5 50	9 5
—	**Newton-Stewart** .... dep.	5 11	8 32	...		1036	...	4 41	7 43
36	Kirkcowan	...	8 43	...		1048	...	4 54	7 54
44½	Glenluce	...	8 56	...		11 2	...	5 10	8 9
47¾	Dunragit 835	...	9 4	...		1112	...	5 18	8 17
50¾	Castle-Kennedy	...	9 12	...		1120	...	5 26	8 25
53¾	**Stranraer Harbour**	5 47	...	...		...	...	...	...
53¼	**Stranraer** .... arr.	6 10	9 19	...		1130	...	5 32	8 30
	To Belfast, 943 dep.	7 0	...	...	1030	1210	...	5 42	...
57¾	Colfin	7 16	...	...	1040	1220	...	5 52	...
60¾	**Portpatrick** .... arr.	7 24	...	...	1050	1230	...	6 2	...

Miles	**Up.**	Week Days. mrn	mrn	mrn	aft	aft	aft
	Portpatrick .... dep.	...	8 45	11 0	2 30	6 30	...
3	Colfin	...	9 0	1110	2 43	6 40	...
7½	**Stranraer** .... arr.	...	9 10	1120	2 54	6 50	...
	From Belfast, 943 dep.	7 30	9 30	Fridays only.	3 40	7 10	9 10
8¾	**Stranraer Harbour**	...	...		...	d	10q3
10	Castle-Kennedy	7 38	9 37		3 48	7 16	...
13	Dunragit	7 45	9 49		3 56	7 25	...
16½	Glenluce	7 55	9 59		4 4	7 33	...
24½	Kirkcowan	8 13	1017		4 24	7 53	...
31	**Newton-Stewart** .... arr.	8 23	1027		4 34	8 3	1040
—	Mls **Whithorn** .... dep.	7 20	9 20		3 30	...	6 40
—	4 Millisle, for Garlieston ..	7 29	9 32		3 39	...	6 48
—	5¼ Sorbie	7 35	9 41		3 45	...	6 53
—	8¼ Whauphill	7 42	9 48		3 52	...	6 59
—	10 Kirkinner	7 47	9 53		3 57	...	7 4
—	12¼ Wigtown	7 54	10 3		4 5	...	7 10
—	19¼ **Newton-Stewart** ... arr.	8 9	1018		4 20	...	7 24
—	**Newton-Stewart** .... dep.	8 29	1037	...	4 41	...	1043
34¼	Palnure	8 35	1044	...	4 49	...	...
37½	Creetown	8 43	1053	...	4 59	...	...
41¾	Dromore	8 54	11 5	...	5 11	...	...
51¾	New Galloway	9 15	1126	...	5 33	...	...
54	Parton	9 22	1132	...	5 39	...	...
57	Crossmichael	9 32	1139	...	5 48	...	...
60¾	**Castle Douglas 839** .... arr.	9 39	1146	...	5 55	...	1127
80½	839 Dumfries .... arr.	1016	1225	...	6 37	...	1159
95¼	885 Lockerbie .... "	...	1 28	...	7 42	...	6g49
163	830 Glasgow (St. Enoch.) ... "	1 25	3 20	...	1015	...	6‡10
171¾	842 " (Central) .... "	...	4 10	...	11 0	...	9,52
170½	848 Edinbro' (Princes St.) .. "	...	4 10	...	1055	...	9z40
113½	831 Carlisle (Cit., G.&S.W.) "	1135	1 28	...	8 3	...	1242
173¾	697 Newcastle (Central) ... "	2 55	4 8	...	11 5	d	2 30
254¼	686 York (N.E.) .... "	6 10	6 36	...	1 15	...	9t19
239	831 Manchester (Victoria) † "	3 32	4 50	...	1230	...	5u15
249½	831 Liverpool (Exchange) † . "	3 30	4 50	...	...	...	5u15
226¼	613 Leeds (Wellington) ..... "	2 25	3 58	...	1130	...	3l56
236¾	831 Manchester (Exchange) "	4 5	6 12	...	1230	i	5 15
241¾	761 " (Victoria) * "	3 40	5 26	...	1217		...
232¼	831 Liverpool (Exchange) * "	3 15	5a32	...	...		...
239	831 " (Lime Street) "	4 15	5 48	...	12 0	...	5 35
341	572 Birmingham (Mid.) ..... "	5 35	7 20	...	3 20	...	7h25
307	413 " (L. N. W.). "	5 3	7 55	...	2 33	...	6 9
424	831 **London** (St. Pancras) ... "	6 30	8 15	...	5 40	...	8qv5
412½	831 " (Euston) .... "	6 20	9 15	...	3 50	...	7 10

a Arrives at 5 48 aft. on Saturdays. *b* Except Sunday nights. d Through Carriages between Newcastle and Stranraer, see pages 696 and 697. *g* Except Sunday mornings; Passengers stay in Dumfries overnight. *h* Arrives at 8 35 mrn. on Sundays. i London Road Station, via Warrington and Stockport. *k* Except Mondays. *l* Arrives at 4 11 mrn. on Sundays. *o* Leaves at 10 5 aft. on Sundays. *q* Through Carriage and Sleeping Car between St. Pancras and Stranraer Harbour. *r* Leaves at 10 15 aft. on Sundays. *t* Arrives at 10 16 mrn. on Sundays. *u* Arrives at 5 30 mrn. on Sundays. *v* Arrives at 8 20 mrn. on Sundays. *z* Leaves at 4 48 aft. on Sundays. * Via Preston. † Via Hellifield. ‡ Arrives at 7 43 mrn. on Sundays.

☞ A Conveyance runs to and from **Garlieston** Village and **Millisle** Station in connection with all Trains.

STRANRAER, CASTLE-KENNEDY, and DUNRAGIT.—Portpatrick and Wigtownshire Joint.

Miles.	**Down.**	Week Days. mrn	mrn	mrn	mrn	aft	aft	aft
	Stranraer ....dep.	7 20	7 30	9 30	1130	3 40	4 15	7 10
	" **Harbour** "	...	...	...	...	...	...	...
2½	Castle-Kennedy ...	7 27	7 38	9 37	1137	3 47	4 22	7 16
5½	**Dunragit** .....arr.	7 35	7 45	9 42	1149	3 53	4 30	7 25

Miles.	**Up.**	Week Days. mrn	mrn	mrn	mrn	aft	aft	aft	aft
	Dunragit ......dep.	8 54	9 4	1112	1143	3 26	5 18	7 25	8 17
3	Castle-Kennedy	9 1	9 12	1120	1152	3 33	5 26	7 32	8 25
5¼	**Stranraer** .....arr.	9 6	9 19	1130	12 0	3 38	5 32	7 37	8 30
6¼	" **Harbour** "	...	...	...	...	...	...	...	...

until October 1964. The line from Stranraer to Portpatrick itself remained open until February 1950, when it became one of the first ex-joint lines to be closed by BR, although it remained for goods as far as Colfin until April 1959. The Whithorn branch closed to passengers in September 1950 and to goods in October 1964.

The London–Stranraer boat-train sleeper services provided a lifeline, and when closure was recommended in the Beeching report there was outrage. Questions were asked in Parliament, and plans were even formulated for the line to be run locally. In response BR argued that Stranraer would still retain its rail connection to Glasgow. The proposed diversion of sleeper services and other through trains via Ayr was seen as an acceptable alternative way of reaching Stranraer, and this finally put paid to the 'Port Road'. The remaining lines closed in June 1965 with the exception of the Challock Junction–Stranraer Harbour section, which still provides part of the link to Glasgow.

Since closure some sections have been absorbed back into the countryside, although a number of the key engineering works remain as important features in the landscape, including viaducts at Big Water of Fleet, Glenluce and Loch Ken.

Left: Passing the junction with the neatly maintained former joint line to Stranraer (curving away to the right), BR Standard Class 4MT 2-6-0 No 76073 approaches Castle Douglas with the 9.25am from Kirkcudbright on 18 April 1965, its driver ready to surrender the single-line token. This location has since been landscaped and developed. *G. Robinson*

London Midland and Scot
Railway Company
(G. & S. W. Section).
TO
SORBI
P. P. & W. RY.,
FROM
DUMFRIES

Left: Cattle imported from Ireland once constituted a valuable source of freight traffic. Here ex-LMS 'Crab' 2-6-0 No 42915 hurries an up livestock special over the Loch Ken Viaduct on 14 July 1956. Consisting of three steel bowstring arches supported by hefty stone piers, the viaduct crosses the narrowest part of the freshwater loch, between Parton and New Galloway. *G. Robin*

Above: The line was used for troop movements and to transport military equipment to and from Northern Ireland. During World War 2 whole divisions at a time used the Stranraer–Larne crossing, and the lengthy single-line sections demanded careful pathing of the numerous additional trains, to avoid congestion. The 'Troubles' in Northern Ireland also resulted in considerable use of the line; here a Stranraer–Woodburn troop train is seen crossing the Loch Ken Viaduct on 16 May 1965. *W. Sellar*

Right: Ex-CR Class 2F 0-6-0 No 57340 calls at Sorbie in the 1950s with the thrice-weekly branch goods from Newton Stewart to Whithorn. The station at Sorbie was located some way north of the village, and passenger services were withdrawn in September 1950, but a creamery near the station continued to generate traffic for the railway until October 1964. The station buildings and stationmaster's house survive today as private dwellings, while the former creamery has found alternative industrial use. *D. Lawrence*

Centre right: London–Belfast timetable, April 1956.

Table **98**		**LONDON—BELFAST** VIA STRANRAER—LARNE				**British Railways**	
		Sunday to Friday nights				**Weekday nights**	
London, Euston............dep.		AR7 30 pm	Belfast, York Road............dep.			5 50 pm	
Stranraer Harbour............arr.		5*45 am	**Larne,** Harbour ....dep.			6 50 pm	
Stranraer, Harbour............dep.		7* 0 am	Stranraer, Harbour ....arr.			8 55 pm	
Larne, Harbour............arr.		9*15 am	Stranraer Harbour ....dep.			10 0 pm	
Belfast, York Road............arr.		10* 5 am	London, Euston...............arr.			A8*10 am	
FARES :—	1st cl. throughout		3rd cl. Rail.	1st cl. Boat	3rd cl. throughout		
	Single	3 Mth. Ret.	Single	3 Mth. Ret.	Single	3 Mth. Ret.	Transfer on Boat from
London—Larne	122/11	221/8	89/10	166/1	78/10	142/5	3rd to 1st class:
London—Belfast......	125/11	224/–	91/8	166/1	80/7	142/5	Single 11/8 Return 23/7
Stranraer—Larne	27/5	54/10	—		15/9	31/3	
Steamer Reservation Tickets not required. * Following day. A Sleeping Car. R Refreshment Car London to Crewe.							

Right: The same train arriving at Whithorn, then the most southerly station in Scotland. The gradients on the branch were quite steep, and the summit was reached by a climb of 1 in 58 on the final approach to Whithorn. Closed along with the rest of the branch in 1964, the station has since been demolished. *D. Lawrence*

Top: All lines remained steam-operated until closure, and in latter years BR Standard Class 6 'Clan' Pacifics were occasional visitors. Here No 72007 *Clan Mackintosh* is seen amid the bleak moorland landscape near Gatehouse of Fleet with a 10-coach Woodburn–Stranraer troop special on 30 May 1965. The locomotive, based at Carlisle Kingmoor shed, would be withdrawn that December. *Derek Cross*

Above: The Big Water of Fleet Viaduct, with its 20 arches, survived closure of the line and, as apparent from this photograph, taken on 1 July 2009, remains an impressive feature of this remote part of Scotland. The location has been used in a number of films, notably the 1935 version of *The Thirty Nine Steps*, based on John Buchan's novel, and *The Five Red Herrings* (1975), a Lord Peter Wimsey mystery by Dorothy L. Sayers. *Author*

Left: The viaduct was built across boggy land, and movement of the structure was detected in 1924. As a result much of the original, mainly stone structure was encased in brick, while the stone arches were strengthened with metal ties and rods. *Author*

Above right: Working its way east from Gatehouse of Fleet, the Port Road track-lifting train, headed by BR/Sulzer Type 2 No D5407, pauses at Lock Skerrow on 12 August 1968. Alongside (right) stands the contractor's locomotive, ready for the next stage of demolition. *Derek Cross*

Caledonian joint railways

The CR was a partner in all the joint lines in Scotland. In the Glasgow area the short Govan and Porterfield branches were, from 1903, run by the Glasgow & Paisley Joint Railway, which was a joint Caledonian/G&SW concern. Both branches closed to regular passenger services in the 1920s, victims of Glasgow's trams. Freight from the remaining King's Inch section of the Porterfield branch ended in July 1964. A freight spur to Prince's Dock, which had the North British Railway as an additional partner, survived until December 1970, while freight on part of the Govan branch lasted until May 1972. The Caledonian and G&SW railways also owned the Glasgow, Barrhead & Kilmarnock Joint line, which included a 5-mile branch to Beith, closed in November 1962, although track to an MoD depot at Giffen remained, unused, in 2009.

Nominally independent, the 8½-mile Kilsyth & Bonnybridge Railway opened in 1888 with staff provided by the CR and NBR. The line provided a link between the two companies, and in 1908 they assumed joint control. The line lost its passenger services in February 1935 and the remaining section closed in December 1964. The CR and NBR also ran the Dumbarton & Balloch Joint Railway, of which a short section at Balloch Pier closed in September 1986. The only other stretch of 'lost' joint line in Scotland the lightly constructed Carmyllie branch of the CR/NBR-owned Dundee & Arbroath Joint Railway; built to serve slate quarries but opened to passengers in 1900, it closed to all traffic in May 1965.

Above: Whilst the Caledonian Railway was a partner in the P&W it was also part-owner, with the HR and NBR, of the Station Hotel at Perth. Opened in 1890, the hotel was used by Queen Victoria, for whom direct access was provided from the platform. The entrance, the outline of which seen here in July 2009, has long been out of use, but the only former joint-railway hotel in Scotland remains open. *Author*

25

County Donegal Railways Joint Committee

There was just one joint narrow-gauge railway, and this was located in the north west of Ireland. The remoteness of the area resulted in the County Donegal Railways Joint Committee being established by the two neighbouring railway companies, which agreed to take over the existing County Donegal Railway to prevent either's expansion into the area it served. Consequently in 1906 the 3ft-gauge CDR lines were purchased jointly by the Northern Counties Committee (itself owned by the MR) and the Great Northern Railway of Ireland — excluding the Strabane–Londonderry section, which competed with the GNR(I)'s own line — under the title of the CDRJC, a name that was retained until the railway closed.

There were no shareholders, and the committee consisted of three members of the GNR(I) and three from the MR. By 1909 it was responsible for the most extensive narrow-gauge network in the United Kingdom, administering some 124½ miles of line from its offices at Stranorlar. Some 91 miles were owned entirely by the committee, and the 14½-mile Strabane–Derry section by the MR, while the 19¼-mile section of the nominally independent Strabane & Letterkenny Railway was also run by the CDRJC.

The committee settled down well, and the railway was capably run in what politically was to become a volatile border area. The railway had its own rolling stock, distinctive geranium-liveried locomotives and a coat of arms. The committee, particularly under

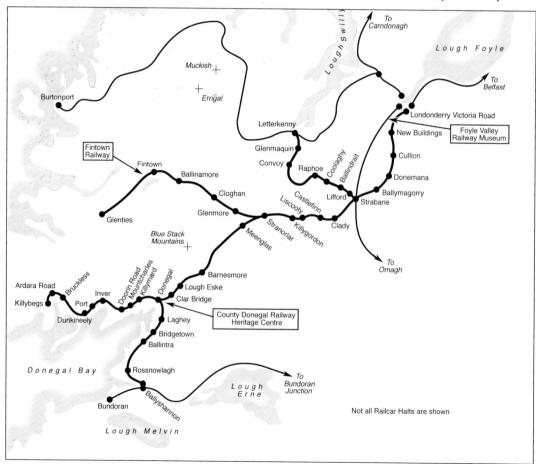

Right: Donegal was a key junction on the 3ft-gauge CDRJC, with four platforms and lines to Killybegs, Ballyshannon and Stranorlar. The busy station is seen here in the 1950s with a mixed train hauled by 2-6-4T *Blanche*, dating from 1912, and passenger railcar No 16, dating from 1936. Note the somersault-type signal and capacious platform shelter. The main stone-built station buildings survive as home to a railway museum. *P. B. Whitehouse*

Below right: The only sizeable intermediate settlement on the Ballyshannon branch was Ballintra. Here 2-6-4T No 4 *Meenglas* calls at the station with a Ballyshannon–Donegal goods on 11 May 1950. Signalling was removed in 1951 as an economy measure, and the signalbox was demolished in 1953, but the stationmaster's house survives, as does the water tower. *W. Camwell*

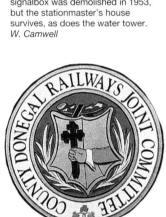

General Manager Henry Forbes, was both thrifty and innovative, pioneering the use of diesel railcars and attracting every type of traffic. Halts were added, bus and train services were integrated, the staff were loyal and the committee seemed to be succeeding, making a profit until World War 2. The committee also aimed to encourage tourism, contributing to a new golf course at Rossnowlagh, but the 'Troubles' wrecked any hotel plans, and the railway was subject to sabotage in this border area between Northern Ireland and the Republic.

Over the years the constituents of the committee changed, the MR's involvement in the Northern Counties Committee becoming the responsibility of the LMS in 1923, and this transferred in 1948 to the Railway Executive (LMR) and in 1953 to the British Transport Commission (LMR). In 1953 the GNR(I) ran out of money and was nationalised, becoming the Great Northern Railway Board. This was a statutory body created by two acts, one in the Republic and one in Northern Ireland, that enabled continued operation of the GNR(I) by a joint committee of the UTA and the CIE. Throughout all the changes they continued to appoint three representatives each to the CDRJC.

As the poor roads and bus services were improved, patronage on the CDRJC lines fell. The Glenties branch closed in 1952, and the formation of the UTA put paid to the Londonderry–Strabane section in 1955. Losses were met by the two sponsoring governments in a ratio of the track mileage in the Republic and Northern Ireland. In 1957, as losses mounted, the committee applied to close the Ballyshannon branch. Objections were still being considered when in May 1959 a formal application was made to close all remaining lines. Permission to close this most attractive line was duly given, and the last joint railway in the British Isles was closed on 30 December 1959. Road freight and buses painted in the distinctive CDRJC livery continued until 1971, when they were taken over by the CIE, and the CDRJC was no more.

Left: Railcar No 20 was the last provided for the CDRJC in 1951 and is seen here at Inver, on 4 September 1957. The joint committee proved to be very good at running the railway economically and was the first to use regular diesel traction in the British Isles. Even the passing loop at Inver was converted into a siding, with just one set of points and less signalling, savings could be made. An early arrival would simply back into the siding to allow passing to take place. *N. Simmons*

Table 23	LONDONDERRY, LETTERKENNY DONEGAL and KILLYBEGS
	County Donegal Joint Committee

	Week Days										Suns.			Week Days								
	a m D	a m	a m		p m	p m	p.m	p.m	p.m	p m	p.m			a.m	a.m	a.m	a.m	a.m		p.m	p.m	p.m	p.m	p.m
Londonderry A.... dep	6 55	9 35	1015	..	1 25	3 50	3 50	5 30	6 45	..	6 15	Killybegs .... dep	..	..	..	7 45	9 27	..	..	1230	3 50	..	..
Strabane............ dep	7 45	10 2	1120	..	2 40	4 55	5 26	6 10	8 0	..	1155	Ballyshannon..... "	..	..	8 0	..	..	..	12 0	4 0	..	..
Letterkenny ...... arr	9*18	..	1232	..	3 52	..	6 47	..	9 15	..	1 17	Donegal .... "	..	..	8 55	1034	..	..	1 42	5 0	..	..
Stranorlar........... "	8 31	1045	1212	..	3 32	5 35	..	6 50	8 40	..	..	Stranorlar........... "	6 45	..	8 45	9 55	1129	..	1 20	2 40	6 5	..	..
Donegal .... "	9 24	..	1 9	..	4 30	6 43	..	7 51	..	..	..	Letterkenny ...... "	..	8 0	..	..	1115	..	..	2 35	5 35	6 57	9 30
Ballyshannon B.. "	1019	..	2 25	..	6 58	8 52	..	8 52	..	..	..	Strabane............ arr	7 28	9 10	9 30	1040	1225	..	2 0	3 25	6 50	8 0	1035
Killybegs C........ "	1035	..	2 35	..	6 17	50	..	9 50	..	..	..	Londonderry A.... arr	9 30	..	..	1135	2 30	..	2 30	5 5	8 25	26	1110

A Foyle Road   B 1 mile to Ballyshannon (G.N.I.) Station   C Station for Carrick (9 miles)   D Mondays and Saturdays only   S or Š Saturdays only
* Dep Strabane 8 10 am   † Arr Strabane 6 36 pm   ‖ Arr Strabane 3 48 pm

Above: CDRJC timetable, April 1955.

Left: Railcar No 20 and a four-wheel box-wagon trailer in the remote countryside of the Barnesmore Gap on 27 September 1957. The heavily graded Barnesmore Gap section also acted on occasions as a funnel for westerly gales. The remote and sparsely populated countryside played a part in the eventual demise of the railway, but ultimately it was deferred permanent-way maintenance during World War 2 and the wider financial difficulties of the joint owners that led to the final downfall of this remarkably innovative joint enterprise. *Hugh Davis*

Right: Terminus of the 19¼-mile line from Strabane, the CDRJC station at Letterkenny opened on 1 January 1909. The station was maintained to a high standard of neatness, as this undated photograph, taken prior to the introduction in the 1930s of the red-and-cream passenger-carriage livery, shows. Adjacent to the CDRJC station and connected by a spur was the Londonderry & Lough Swilly Railway station.
Ian Allan Library

Right: The CDRJC station at Letterkenny closed with effect from 1 January 1960 and is seen here after lifting of the track, which was completed by the end of August 1960. The platform and canopy are still intact, and a covered wagon has been marooned at one of the platforms. The yard was still in use for road goods traffic when the photograph was taken. The booking office was retained and used as part of a bus depot on the site.
D. Lawrence

Right: Crest of the Great Northern Railway Board, which joint undertaking was formed to run the bankrupt GNR(I). The Board had five nominees from the UTA, from Northern Ireland, and five from CIE, from the Republic, resulting in a rare instance of a railway run jointly by the governments of two countries. *Author*

Far right: There are many surviving traces of the CDRJC, including the majority of the stone bridges, although the metal bridges have been dismantled for scrap. This view of the derelict remains of the water tower at Inver, on the Donegal–Killybegs line, was recorded in August 2005. The former station buildings also remain here, as they do at many other locations on the former joint railway. *Author*

Many joint railways are fondly remembered, and a number of sections of formerly joint line have been reopened. Memorabilia has also been preserved in numerous museums, as the uniqueness of joint railways has always been of great interest, in particular their signs. Some excellent replicas have been produced, but some fascinating originals survive. Rare and original cast-iron signs, kept at Winchcombe Railway Museum in Gloucestershire, are illustrated in this chapter.

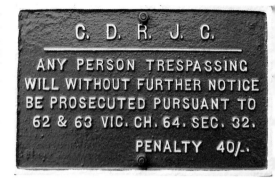

County Donegal Railways Joint Committee

There are various remains of this delightful narrow-gauge line in Ireland. The Fintown Railway runs for 3 miles along the shores of Lough Finn, on the former Glenties branch. Stock and memorabilia are preserved at the County Donegal Railway Restoration Society, housed at Donegal station. The Foyle Valley Railway Museum at Derry is currently closed, but stock and artefacts can be found at the Ulster Folk & Transport Museum at Cultra, County Down. A section of line was re-laid at Inver in 2009 to mark the 50th anniversary of the closure

Left: The original platform sign from Strabane station has been preserved at the Ulster Folk & Transport Museum at Cultra, in Northern Ireland. Some of the connecting destinations were removed from the sign as lines closed, but these have now been replaced. The museum also houses a locomotive and numerous other exhibits from the CDRJC. This photograph was taken in August 2005. *Author's collection*

Severn & Wye Joint Railway

In Gloucestershire the 4¼-mile Lydney Junction–Parkend section of the erstwhile S&W joint railway has been restored by the Dean Forest Railway and, reflecting the thickly wooded nature of the area, is sometimes known as the 'Friendly Forest Line'.

Right: A replica LMS 'target' station name sign, seen at Lydney Junction, on the former Severn & Wye Joint Railway, in April 2009. The station is now the southern terminus of the preserved Dean Forest Railway. The original LMS name signs of this design were of a special reflective alloy and made by Hawkseye. *Author*

Metropolitan & Great Central Joint Committee

Much of this line remains open, including the freight-only route north of Aylesbury through Quainton Road station. However, the ex-MetGC station and yard at Quainton Road have been preserved as the Buckinghamshire Railway Centre. Much of the trackbed of the jointly run tramway to Brill has become a footpath.

Right: A new Quainton Road station sign, but consisting of letters traditionally screwed onto a wooden base and seen here in September 1997. The platform for the Brill Tramway is to the left of this view, behind the flowers, on this ex-Metropolitan & Great Central Joint Committee line. The site is now occupied by the Buckinghamshire Railway Centre. *Author*

Midland & Great Northern Joint Railway

The North Norfolk Railway runs the 5½-mile 'Poppy Line' between Sheringham and Holt, while the William Marriott Museum at Holt station houses M&GN memorabilia. Ambitious plans to extend the line to Melton Constable, as part of a Norfolk orbital railway, are under tentative consideration. In addition Whitwell & Reepham station, on the former Norwich–Melton Constable line, has been preserved, and a short running line opened.

Left: The reconstructed station at Holt is now the terminus of the North Norfolk Railway from Sheringham. The replica wooden sign, seen here in April 2009, resembles one of the black-and-white-painted concrete signs made at Melton Constable and at one time commonplace throughout the M&GN system. *Author*

Below right: The ex-M&GN station at Whitwell & Reepham is now preserved and open to the public.

Ashby & Nuneaton Joint Railway

The station at Shackerstone, Leicestershire, where the joint railway had its headquarters, has been restored, and a railway museum here contains a large amount of memorabilia. The 4¾-mile Shackerstone–Shenton section of line has been reopened and, due to its proximity to Bosworth Field, where Henry VII was victorious in battle, is known today as the Battlefield Line Railway.

Left: Replica station sign, seen in August 2008, on the former Ashby & Nuneaton Joint Railway, nowadays part of the Battlefield Line Railway. From Shenton station a walk leads to the site of the Battle of Bosworth Field. *Author*

Somerset & Dorset Joint Railway

The S&D was greatly missed after closure, and the Somerset & Dorset Railway Trust has a considerable collection of memorabilia at Washford station, on the West Somerset Railway, which line is home to one of the S&D's two surviving 2-8-0 locomotives. The Mendip Main Line Project, based at Midsomer Norton

South station, has ambitious long-term plans to reopen the S&D south to Chilcompton and north to Radstock. There is also the restored S&D station at Shillingstone, which has a collection of memorabilia and a short running line, while at Templecombe miniature trains run on the Gartell Light Railway using a ½-mile section of the S&D trackbed.

Right: The S&D Mendip Main Line Project is based Midsomer Norton South station, which has been preserved and is now open to the public.

Left: At the West Somerset Railway's Washford station, home to the S&D Railway Trust, a Southern Railway wooden-framed green-and-white enamel sign from Wincanton contrasts with a Southern Region sign for Templecombe. The site houses many relics from the S&D, along with Class 7F 2-8-0 No 88 and three former S&D coaches. *Author*

GC AND NS JOINT RAILWAY

NOTICE IS HEREBY GIVEN THAT ANY PERSON WHO SHALL TRESPASS UPON ANY OF THE RAILWAYS OF THE COMPANY IN SUCH A MANNER AS TO EXPOSE HIMSELF TO DANGER OR RISK OF DANGER THEREBY RENDERS HIMSELF LIABLE TO A PENALTY NOT EXCEEDING FORTY SHILLINGS OR IN DEFAULT ONE MONTH'S IMPRISONMENT

BY ORDER

GN. NE & L&Y JOINT RAILWAY

PUBLIC WARNING NOT TO TRESPASS

PERSONS TRESPASSING UPON ANY RAILWAYS BELONGING OR LEASED TO OR WORKED BY THE GREAT NORTHERN RAILWAY COMPANY SOLELY OR IN CONJUNCTION WITH ANY OTHER COMPANY OR COMPANIES, ARE LIABLE TO A PENALTY OF FORTY SHILLINGS UNDER THE GREAT NORTHERN RAILWAY ACT 1896, AND IN ACCORDANCE WITH THE PROVISIONS OF THE SAID ACT PUBLIC WARNING IS HEREBY GIVEN TO ALL PERSONS NOT TO TRESPASS UPON THE SAID RAILWAYS.

KING'S CROSS. JULY 1896.   BY ORDER.

SOMERSET AND DORSET JOINT LINE. TRESPASSING ON THE RAILWAY.

NOTICE IS HEREBY GIVEN THAT UNDER THE PROVISIONS OF THE 37TH SECTION OF THE SOUTH WESTERN RAILWAY ACT, 1902, ANY PERSON WHO SHALL TRESPASS UPON ANY OF THE LINES OF RAILWAY BELONGING OR LEASED TO OR WORKED BY THE SOUTH WESTERN RAILWAY COMPANY IN CONJUNCTION WITH THE MIDLAND RAILWAY COMPANY, SHALL ON CONVICTION BE LIABLE TO A PENALTY NOT EXCEEDING 40/- & PUBLIC WARNING IS HEREBY GIVEN TO PERSONS NOT TO TRESPASS UPON THE RAILWAY.

DATED THIS 5TH DAY OF AUGUST 1903
GODFREY KNIGHT, } JOINT SECRETARIES.
WILLIAM CLOWER,

LONDON & NORTH WESTERN & FURNESS JOINT RAILWAYS. NOTICE.

EXTRACT FROM 8 VIC. CAP. 20 SEC. 75 IF ANY PERSON OMIT TO SHUT AND FASTEN ANY GATE SET UP AT EITHER SIDE OF THE RAILWAY FOR THE ACCOMMODATION OF THE OWNERS OR OCCUPIERS OF THE ADJOINING LANDS AS SOON AS HE AND THE CARRIAGE, CATTLE, OR OTHER ANIMALS UNDER HIS CARE HAVE PASSED THROUGH THE SAME, HE SHALL FORFIT FOR EVERY SUCH OFFENCE ANY SUM NOT EXCEEDING FORTY SHILLINGS.

EUSTON STATION   BY ORDER.
1ST NOVEMBER, 1883.

N S J R   NOTICE

ANY PERSON FOUND TRESPASSING OR THROWING RUBBISH OF ANY KIND ON TO THE RAILWAY COMPANY'S PROPERTY WILL BE PROSECUTED

0.32

DUNDEE & ARBROATH JOINT RAILWAY

WARNING TO TRESPASSERS

THE LONDON & NORTH EASTERN, AND LONDON MIDLAND & SCOTTISH RAILWAY COMPANIES HEREBY GIVE WARNING TO ALL PERSONS NOT TO TRESPASS UPON ANY OF THE RAILWAYS, STATIONS, WORKS LANDS OR PROPERTY BELONGING TO OR WORKED BY THE TWO COMPANIES. TRESPASSERS ARE LIABLE TO A FINE OR IMPRISONMENT FOR EVERY OFFENCE.

BY ORDER

LANCASHIRE & YORKSHIRE AND LONDON AND NORTH WESTERN JOINT LINES CAUTION

PERSONS TRESPASSING UPON THE RAILWAYS BELONGING JOINTLY TO THE LANCASHIRE & YORKSHIRE AND LONDON & NORTH WESTERN RAILWAY COMPANIES, AND PERSONS TRESPASSING UPON THE STATIONS, WORKS, LANDS OR PROPERTY CONNECTED WITH SUCH RAILWAYS ARE LIABLE TO A PENALTY OF FORTY SHILLINGS AND IN ACCORDANCE WITH THE PROVISIONS OF THE LANCASHIRE & YORKSHIRE RAILWAY ACT 1884, AND THE LONDON & NORTH WESTERN RAILWAY ADDITIONAL POWERS ACT 1883, PUBLIC WARNING IS HEREBY GIVEN TO ALL PERSONS NOT TO TRESPASS UPON THE SAID RAILWAYS, STATIONS, WORKS, LANDS OR PROPERTY.

SECRETARY'S OFFICE   BY ORDER.
FLEET .... 1884.

H & B & G C JOINT COMMITTEE BEWARE OF THE TRAINS

THE GREAT NORTHERN AND LONDON AND NORTH WESTERN JOINT COMMITTEE,

CAUTION

PERSONS TRESPASSING UPON THE RAILWAYS BELONGING TO THE GREAT NORTHERN AND LONDON & NORTH WESTERN JOINT COMMITTEE, AND ANY PERSONS TRESPASSING UPON THE STATIONS CONNECTED WITH SUCH RAILWAYS, ARE LIABLE TO A PENALTY OF FORTY SHILLINGS, UNDER THE LONDON & NORTH WESTERN RAILWAY ADDITIONAL POWERS ACT, 1883, AND IN ACCORDANCE WITH THE PROVISIONS OF THE SAID ACT PUBLIC WARNING IS HEREBY GIVEN TO ALL PERSONS NOT TO TRESPASS UPON THE SAID RAILWAYS OR STATIONS.

FEBRUARY, 1885.   BY ORDER.

SEVERN AND WYE JOINT RAILWAY.

WARNING IS GIVEN AGAINST THE DANGEROUS PRACTICE OF PROPPING UP THE DOORS OF MERCHANDISE TRUCKS FOR THE SUPPORT OF COAL WEIGHING MACHINES, FOR LOADING OR UNLOADING TRAFFIC, OR FOR ANY OTHER PURPOSE. THE SEVERN AND WYE JOINT RAILWAY COMPANY GIVE NOTICE THAT SUCH PRACTICE IS PROHIBITED, AND ANY PERSON DISREGARDING THIS CAUTION WILL BE HELD RESPONSIBLE FOR INJURY OR DAMAGE THAT MAY RESULT.

JNO. A. CARTER.
LYDNEY.   TRAFFIC MANAGER.

G.W. & R. R Y

NOTICE IS HEREBY GIVEN THAT ALL PERSONS FOUND TRESPASSING ON THE LINE OF THIS RAILWAY, OR ON THE LAND ADJACENT THERETO BELONGING TO THE COMPANIES, OR DESTROYING OR INJURING THE FENCES THEREOF, WILL BE PROSECUTED.

BY ORDER

While many sections of ex-joint lines still remain open, it can be seen that a number of closed lines have been preserved and even now display their peculiar brand of distinctiveness, echoing still to the sound of steam and smoke, while others provide delightful footpaths, cycleways, nature reserves and even roads. In all cases they remain a particularly interesting aspect of Britain's lost railways.